Roosevelt Field

World's Premier Airport

by
Joshua Stoff
&
William Camp

Roosevelt Field
World's Premier Airport

by
Joshua Stoff
&
William Camp

Published as part of the
"Aviation Heritage Library Series"
by

SunShine House, Inc.
P.O. Box 2065
Terre Haute, IN 47802
© Copyright 1992 SunShine House, Inc.

(812) 232-3076

First Edition, First Printing
Printed in the United States of America
ISBN 0-943691-06-0

The Aviation Heritage Library Series is published to preserve, for future generations, the history of the men and women, and of their airplanes, during the era of the Golden Years of Aviation. The books in the series include:

The Welch Airplane Story by Drina Welch Abel
It's a Funk! by G. Dale Beach
The Luscombe Story by John C. Swick
The Earhart Disappearance - The British Connection by James A. Donahue
Ryan Sport Trainer by Dorr Carpenter
Aeronca — Best of Paul Matt
Ryan Broughams and Their Builders by William Wagner
The Corsair and other— Aeroplanes Vought by Gerald P. Moran
Peanut Power by Bill Hannan
Paul Matt Scale Airplane Drawings, Vol. 1
Paul Matt Scale Airplane Drawings, Vol. 2
Roosevelt Field — World's Premier Airport by Joshua Stoff & William Camp
WACO — Symbol of Courage & Excellence by Fred Kobernuss

About the Authors

Joshua Stoff received his Masters Degree in Museum Studies from the University of Toronto. He is Air & Space Curator at the Cradle of Aviation Museum, Garden City, New York.

Joshua has authored six other books dealing with aviation and space history.

He enjoys flying antique aircraft and is supervising the restoration of various antique aircraft at the museum.

William Camp received his degree in History from the College of William and Mary and has been a curator at Long Island's Cradle of Aviation Museum since 1985.

Joshua Stoff & William Camp

About the Book

Upon completing this work, we realized that no history of a particular airfield like this has ever been published. It is simply the most definitive account published of any airport anywhere. This is really saying something! The history of this one field can trace the history of aviation from its earliest days to the present era. This was certainly a very unusual, very colorful and very exciting airfield.

We also included quite a few period quotations in order to add color to the times. We believe this book will be of interest to anyone who likes old airplanes.

The real heart of the project are the 300 rare, wonderful photos — each carefully selected after sorting through about 1500. We selected based on the quality of the picture, its rarity, and its interest.

The map on the next page helps to identify the layout of Roosevelt Field.

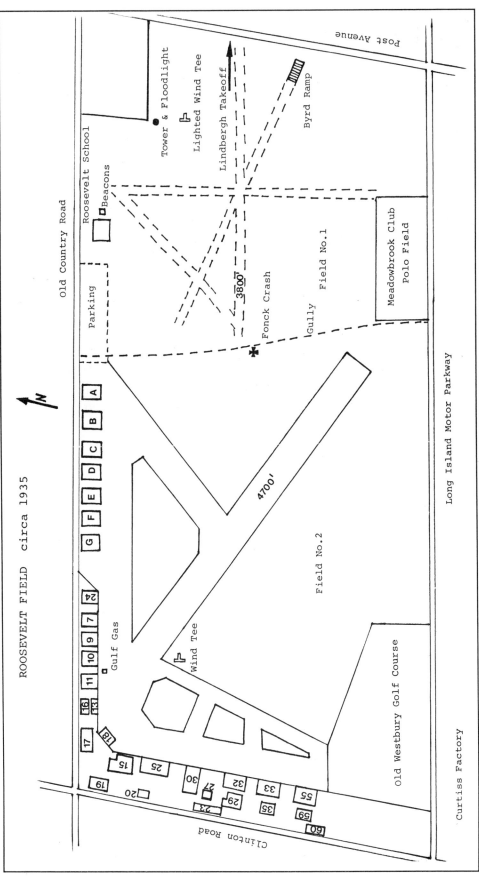

Roosevelt Field Buildings

7 Luscombe Sales
9 Waco Sales
10 Steinman-Rintoul
11 Plane Owners Service, Fox News
13 Aircraft Radio Instrument Training, Waco Sales, Aeronautical Radio
15 Roosevelt Field Inn
16 Police Office, Drennan Photography, (Spirit of St. Louis stored here)
17 Aero Trades
18 Operations Office
19 Waco, Engine Air Service
20 Air Transport Equipment
23 Roosevelt Field Museum
24 Gulf
25 Air Associates
27 Lear Inc.
29 Roosevelt Aviation School
30 Roosevelt Aviation School
32 Dept. of Commerce, Munch & Romeo, Rappoport
33 Reich Air Service, Annette Gipson, Belfair
35 Joe Crane
55 Roger Wolfe Kahn (ROWEKA)
59 Roosevelt Aviation School
60 Roosevelt Aviation School

Concrete Hangars

A Atlantic Aviation Sales, Beechcraft, Cessna
B Safair School
C Engine Air, Leech Inc. (Stinson), Beckwith Havens (Fairchild), Licon Airways
D Monocoupe, Cordova-McKenna Aircraft Sales
E Aeronautical Radio Co., Howard Sales
F Foley, Pester, Davis, Beechcraft, Instruction & Charter
G Potter Upholstery, Gregor

Introduction

Roosevelt Field prospered to become the veritable reflection of aviation's 'Golden Age' for three reasons:

1) The land upon which the airport was developed was entirely suited to the technical abilities of aircraft for over forty years.
2) Roosevelt Field grew in a suburban county which retained its rural character shortly after the turn of the century, yet the Field benefited from visitor accessibility by road and rail transport.
3) The airport for a time serviced the largest metropolitan area in the nation and grew as a result of its proximity to New York's financial and human resources.

As Glenn Curtiss discovered, the flat and unobstructed Hempstead Plains were golden for flying in the days before World War I. Aviation centers sprouted at Belmont Park, Garden City Estates, Mineola, and on Roosevelt Field's future site at the Hempstead Plains aerodrome. The civilian aviation establishment planted in 1911 at the Hempstead Plains field provided the military with a base outline when war began in 1914. After the war, the military exploited a larger parcel of the Plains due south of the original aerodrome, and the wartime move of the Curtiss Engineering Corporation assured the articulation of a first-rate test field for Curtiss products and for the home base of the Curtiss Flying Service. The longer stretches of turf to the east on Roosevelt Field's ill-defined runways were flown from by all the great flights in 1927.

The consolidation of Curtiss and Roosevelt Fields in 1929 guaranteed the epithet 'World's Premier Airport,' but ironically the more significant record-breaking flights of the 1930s took off from and landed on the larger runways of Floyd Bennett Field in Brooklyn. Before World War II the original Roosevelt Field was developed as an automobile racetrack and acreage to the south became a polo field. Nonetheless, the quaint and well-planned setting of the aeronautical service buildings; the modern form of the concrete hangars along Old Country Road; the technically progressive lighting, radio, and weather installations; all offered unrivaled facilities for those businesses which provided services while flying airplanes and for private pilots.

Beginning with the first aerial excursions over the Hempstead Plains visitors flocked to see for the first time an airplane in flight; but this could have been true throughout the 1920s when it was not uncommon for even a young adult to see his or her first airplane. The Long Island Rail Road covered the distance between the airport and midtown Manhattan in less than forty-five minutes, and suburban Long Island was always considered a picturesque place about which one might pleasurably cycle or drive. Roosevelt Field was visible and accessible to the touring public from the start of the century.

Long Island life has always been particularly shaded by the towers of Manhattan, and this was no less true in regard to aviation. New York's financial and human resources continuously propelled aeronautical activity at Roosevelt Field; and its vital cultural center also provided the airport with a wealthy crop of potential airplane buyers, lessors, and air travelers.

Though the pre-eminence of Roosevelt Field during the 'Golden Age' was manifest by the presence at the field of every significant aeronautical trend, the collected photographs presented here depict the more elusive, day-to-day life of an airport in the midst of a nation which was following the ever-widening, wonderful and exciting world of everything aeronautical.

During this time Roosevelt Field, and subsequent historians, were very fortunate in that a dedicated news photographer named John Drennan worked on the field. Assigned to the airport in 1929, Drennan remained until its final days. He captured the famous pilots and planes, but gave full treatment to Roosevelt's daily life as well. Of the total collection of photographs included herein, two-thirds are the work of Drennan. In an attempt to extend our feeling of indebtedness to the late Mr. Drennan, we have tried to assemble a survey of his photos in a manner which catalogs Roosevelt Field's history and serves as an expression of our gratitude to the photographer whose work was left us to display fittingly.

As a few words about names are in order: the northwest corner of Roosevelt Field was formed by the intersection of east-west Old Country Road and north-south Clinton Road. If one were to have traveled west one mile to Mineola, one would have arrived at the flying site used by Glenn Curtiss in 1909. This was the Mineola flying field. The Hempstead Plains at the corner of Old Country and Clinton were the site of the 1911 Moisant School. Throughout the prewar period the aerodrome was known as the Hempstead Plains aviation field. During World War I the field then became Hazelhurst Field, although before and after the declaration of war by the U.S. in 1917, this site was also loosely termed Mineola, perhaps because so many servicemen arrived at the field after making the last train stop at the Mineola station. After the death of Quentin Roosevelt in 1918 the eastern portion became known as Roosevelt Field. Regardless of the predominantly level expanse of the Plains, Roosevelt Field was ten to fifteen feet greater in elevation than Hazelhurst, and the two were separated by a gully which gave the appearance to an eastward gazing viewer of Roosevelt Field being a plateau. In 1920 the Curtiss company purchased Hazelhurst and renamed it Curtiss Field. In 1929, Curtiss and Roosevelt Fields were combined and only the latter name was retained.

In the last quarter of the twentieth century the land area of Roosevelt Field has been extensively developed into a complete variety of business enterprises, and the name remains to adorn one of the nation's quintessential postwar shopping malls. The County of Nassau's Division of Museum Services exhibits its air and spacecraft collection in two hangars on adjacent Mitchel Field, and historic materials have been continuously gathered in order to interpret Roosevelt Field the airport to future generations. An outdoor abstract sculpture called 'Spirit' commemorates the May 1927 Lindbergh flight, but nothing on the site of the original Roosevelt Field marks the take-off runways of 1927's great flights. There is poignancy to the fact that a place once so glorious has so utterly disappeared.

Acknowledgments

*The authors wish to acknowledge
the kind and perceptive assistance of
Messrs. Jim Boss, George Dade, & Lynn McDonald*

Photo Credits

The authors wish to acknowledge the photographic contributions to this book. All photographs are courtesy of the Nassau County Museum, unless otherwise noted. Additional photographs are courtesy of Aviation Heritage/SunShine House, Inc., Henry Newell, Henry Liese, William Wait, Jim Boss, Joseph Burt, Bill Wildhagen, and Frank Strnad.

Roosevelt Field
World's Premier Airport

Contents

Chapter One
The Hempstead Plains
Pre WWI

Glenn H. Curtiss in the 'Golden Flyer,' Mineola flying field, 1909.

In 1909, an airplane for the first time took off from and landed upon the nearly flat and nearly treeless geologic prairie known as the Hempstead Plains (an expanse roughly sixteen miles in length and four miles in width), located in suburban Nassau County, Long Island, New York. The year before, the airplane was proven in flight in the course of public demonstrations both in the United States and in Europe. Wilbur Wright astounded the French with his demonstrations in 1908 near Le Mans. The Wright brothers, of course, had achieved the first manned, powered, controlled, and sustained flight on December 17, 1903, but their success was ignored. Later, Orville Wright attempted to explain the world's initial indifference to the invention of the century:

"You ask me why it was that the public took so little notice of our 1903 flights and not until 1908 awoke to the fact that human flights had been accomplished. I think it was mainly due to the fact that human flight was generally looked upon as an impossibility and that scarcely anyone believed in it until he actually saw it with his own eyes."[1]

Along with the Wright demonstrations in 1908, and of greater relevance to our Long Island story, were the activities of the Aerial Experiment Association. On March 12, 1908, the A.E.A.'s pusher biplane, the 'Red Wing,' made the first public flight of an airplane in the United States at Lake Keuka, New York. The A.E.A. was chaired by Alexander Graham Bell; its executive manager was Glenn H. Curtiss, a love-mate of speed and a motorcycle engine manufacturer who had been drawn to the infant art of aeronautics after having received a request to construct a powerplant for a dirigible airship. As the Wrights prepared for demonstrations in the U. S. and in Europe, the work of the A.E.A. continued unabated. On July 4, 1908, Curtiss captured the *Scientific American* trophy for the first public fight of one kilometer while flying the Association's 'June Bug,' the next to last experimental aircraft produced by the A.E.A. With the successful flights of the 'Silver Dart,' the first powered, heavier-than-air craft to fly in Canada, the A.E.A. disbanded. But through his successful endeavors, Curtiss had defined his destiny of litigation, fame, and fortune. His skills as an airplane manufacturer were soon in demand.

New York's metropolitan inhabitants were to witness the airplane for the first time in August, 1908, when Henri Farman was invited to Long Island to give a flying exhibition. On January 13, 1908, Farman, in his Voisin biplane, had completed a one kilometer flight on a closed circuitous course at Issy-les-Moulineaux outside Paris. Farman's reputation preceded him and he was paid well for his visit to the United States, but inclement weather, public indifference, and an unsatisfactory performance by his machine accrued to a failed exhibition. Farman returned to Europe convinced that his American tour had been a mistake. At this time, racetracks appeared superficially to provide the facilities requisite for flight demonstrations, and Farman, in fact, had made his abbreviated hops at the Brighton Beach racetrack in Brooklyn. Also, in 1908, another previously established sporting ground was used by New York's indigenous aerial experimenters, the Morris Park racetrack in the Bronx.

The Aeronautic Society of New York began occupying the grounds at Morris Park in August, 1908. The Society had splintered from the Aero Club of New York when the parent organization expressed resistance to steering its focus upon aeronautical endeavors of a scientific nature. When the Aeronautic Society incorporated in July, 1908, it was attempting to distinguish its promotion of empirical work from the social basis of the Aero Club. Morris Park was chosen because it appeared to offer fine grounds for servicing the Society's flight experiments and for providing an attractive site to which New York's denizens could travel with ease by trolley or subway.

Though the skeptical press voiced its derision, the Aeronautic Society continued its work at Morris Park and sought to expand its activities to essay real progress in the aeronautical art. Its boldest move occurred on January 21, 1909, when the Society completed a contract with Glenn Curtiss by which Curtiss was to deliver an airplane of his own design and manufacture. Doubtless that Curtiss's successes with the A.E.A. launched his independent enterprises and made him attractive to the Society. In regard to the contract made with Curtiss, the Aeronautic Society was convinced of its foresight:

"There can be no question that this trip by the Society, viewed even in its simplest form, as a business transaction only, was an historic and most interesting event. This commission constituted the first

purchase of an airplane ever made by an aeronautic society. It was the first commercial transaction of the sort ever made in America. The machine to be built would be the first flying machine ever made to order and for sale in this country. . . it was in fact the actual beginning of the airplane industry in the United States." [2]

In June, 1909, the Aeronautic Society hosted, after distressing delays, an exhibition at Morris Park, at which the Curtiss machine and the inventions created under the Society's auspices were to be flown. Again, the public expected more than the achievements provided, and the Curtiss machine, though beautiful and precisely what had been ordered, was viewed suspiciously given the confining limitations of Morris Park. Curtiss then sought a more suitable flying ground over which he wished to prove the merits of his production and to practice more effectively for his upcoming engagement in the air meet at Rheims, France. Curtiss was brought to Long Island to be shown the expansive Hempstead Plains, which were suggested to him as possessing all the requirements for safe flight tests. After receiving authority from the Aeronautic Society, Curtiss shipped the pusher biplane to Mineola, an act which initiated flying on the Hempstead Plains for the next fifty years. On July 10, Curtiss, from Mineola, wrote to the Wright brothers:

"The exhibition (Morris Park), however, did not pan out well and they have not as yet taken the machine. We have seized the opportunity to secure some trials on Long Island where there are better grounds. We have not before made any attempts at long flights and I am anxious to experiment on these lines." [3]

The Herring-Curtiss 'Golden Flyer' was a pusher biplane powered by a Curtiss 4-cylinder vertical engine. At Mineola, it was hangared in a tent situated for this purpose near the fairgrounds of the provincial agricultural society. Pioneer aeronautical engineer Grover Loening came to Mineola to view the 'Golden Flyer', and he included it in his catalogue of *Monoplanes and Biplanes* published in 1911. Loening noted that "no other type has been as widely imitated by amateurs in this country as the Curtiss." [4]

Certainly Curtiss wished to demonstrate admirably the abilities of his 'Golden Flyer' to the purchasing Aeronautic Society, and indeed he instructed two members of the Society when at Mineola. But in coming to Long Island, Curtiss was also availing himself of added flying time in the weeks before his competitive participation in the Rheims meet. *The Hempstead Sentinel* for July 15, reported:

"Glenn Curtiss, who is making experiments with the airplane, made an ascent with his machine Wednesday morning, on the Plains east of the fair-

'Golden Flyer,' Mineola flying field, 1909.

grounds. He went east to Meadowbrook and back and circled around several times when he alighted, finding that a bolt had broken. Flights will be made every day that conditions are favorable." [5]

On July 16, Curtiss, "in a deliberate practice flight for Rheims, circled ten times for a total of 15 miles in 23 minutes—his longest and best performance to date. He also reached his highest altitude, 50 feet." [6]

Buoyant over his most assured flight, Curtiss arranged the following day for officials to witness his attempt for the *Scientific American* trophy for a flight of 25 kilometers. "A flip of the propeller and he was off again at 5:23 am for the big event, with three gallons of gasoline sloshing in the tank. Round and round the corner he buzzed, at an average altitude of 15 to 25 feet." [7] Three thousand persons awaited the early morning flight and Curtiss thrilled them all with his circuits totaling 25 miles and his flying time of over 52 minutes. He won the *Scientific American* trophy easily and he faced no serious threat to his record for the remainder of 1909.

In order to complete his obligation to the Aeronautic Society, Curtiss instructed two of the Society's members on the 'Golden Flyer': Charles Willard and Alexander Williams. To Willard credit is given for the first cross-country flight over the Plains, a distance of 12 miles. Later, Willard proudly related his experiences as one of the world's first flight students:

"We were on the Hempstead Plains, Long Island, between Mineola and Garden City, a site destined to become Curtiss Field and ultimately Roosevelt Field. Earlier, Curtiss had taken the plane on a test hop. Now, sitting beside me on the wing, he was demonstrating cautious movements of the controls. He

'Golden Flyer,' Mineola flying field, 1909.

advised little movement, just fly straight and level and then land. . . After a run of about 200 feet the 'Golden Flyer' lifted and I rose to about 10 feet. I held her at this level, flying between two country roads about a half mile apart with perhaps fifty automobiles parked at the other end."[8]

Willard then alighted in an anxious though uneventful landing.

The Society's other student pilot, Alexander Williams, was less fortunate. After a stall at 50 feet, Williams and the 'Golden Flyer' fell to the Plains. Both pilot and plane suffered injuries. Williams avoided death, but not broken limbs, and Curtiss assessed the damage to the aircraft as remedial. Inspection of the 'Golden Flyer' revealed the need for new parts, for which reason Curtiss returned to his home at Hammondsport, New York. While there, he completed work on his Rheims machine previous to its shipment to France for the international meet. Curtiss then returned to Mineola to refurbish the 'Golden Flyer' and to terminate formally his work for the Aeronautic Society by receiving his final payment. Later in August, Willard was back at the 'Flyer's' controls. For his cross-country flight over Mineola, Garden City, Westbury, and Hicksville, Willard was accompanied on the ground by a parade of automobiles. A broken camshaft forced Willard into a deadstick landing a few miles shy of his take-off mark, but his flight, nevertheless, carried him 12 miles in 19 minutes and was enough to outdistance the cross-country flight made by Orville Wright two weeks earlier.

The victory by Glenn Curtiss in the Gordon Bennett race at Rheims assured the United States of hosting the event in 1910. *The Hempstead Sentinel* mused on September 23, 1909:

"Just where the next aviation meet will be held is a speculative question at present. Washington, Cincinnati, St. Louis, Chicago, and Philadelphia are all anxious to secure this aviation prize of the year, and from some of them tentative propositions have already been made to the Aero Club of America. Meanwhile the Directors of the Club are saying nothing. Their personal preference is strongly for New York, for no better aviation field could be obtained than on the Hempstead Plains."[9]

Until the end of 1909, the biplane configuration was the predominant design to fly in the United States. On July 25, 1909, Louis Bleriot made the first airplane flight across the English Channel in his Model XI, a monoplane which in a short time would be found throughout the aeronautical world. In December, 1909, the first American monoplane was flown at the Mineola flying field by Dr. Henry Walden, a dentist by profession, who was a member of the Aeronautic Society and another fledgling who departed the inappropriate Morris Park for the friendlier expanse of the Hempstead Plains:

"My first plane took shape in 1908. It was a tandem biplane. It looked like two biplanes with an open fuselage between. Neither of the two biplane models I built (the Walden I and II) ever flew. . . These experiments were carried out at the Morris Park field in the Bronx, a busy center of flying activities in the early days. The plains of central Long Island had attracted the attention of aviation people, and in 1909 I moved out to the field east of the present Mineola fairgrounds. Late in 1909 I was making straightaway flights with the Walden III, which became known as the first successful American monoplane."[10]

Dr. Walden continued to fly his monoplane until it was wrecked on August 3, 1910. He had added a ten-gallon fuel tank to permit an extended cross-country flight, which perhaps precipitated the monoplane's demise, but Walden attributed the crash to structural failure. The Walden III had made only straightaway flights up to this time, so in anticipation of his extended flight trials, Dr. Walden surveyed the Mineola flying grounds in case of having to alight upon slightest provocation:

Gold Bug Hotel across from Mineola flying field, frequented by Curtiss and other early aviators on Long Island, circa 1910.

Walden monoplane, first successful American monoplane, 1910.

"The only apparent obstacle was the motor parkway embankment which trailed along the eastern limits of our field. The section beyond, which is Roosevelt Field today, we called the graveyard. We honestly feared it because of previous crashes in that area."[11]

Walden survived the August wreck and went on to construct nine other models.

The wonderfully successful aviation tournament held at Rheims inspired a proliferation of flying meets throughout 1910, though the International Meet at Belmont Park in October was the premier American event. Throughout the year, aviation activity on Long Island centered about the Mineola Flying Field next to the grounds of the agricultural society. One mile to the east, the Hempstead Plains continued its treeless and unobstructed expanse, and this larger tract was indeed more suitable than the terrain at Mineola, which was narrow and hemmed by roads in anticipation of building development. By June, 1910, a stalwart contingent was clamoring for the International Meet to be held on the larger parcel of the Hempstead Plains, the precise site of which was to become Roosevelt Field:

"The field is about two miles long and one mile in width. It has been examined by Wilbur Wright, Charles K. Hamilton, Louis Paulhan, Glenn H. Curtiss, Clifford B. Harmon, and several other aviators, and pronounced excellent. Mr. Wright said that it probably was the most admirable site for an international meet that could be found in the United States.

Engineers are now at work there, and as soon as the proper surveys have been completed and contracts let a large force of men will be put to work erecting grandstands and such other buildings as will be needed. The field will be fenced in and parking spaces for more than 10,000 automobiles will be produced. The grandstands will have a seating capacity of from 30,000 to 40,000 people. Sheds for aviators, a clubhouse, and other structures will be built also."[12]

Ultimately, the decision to host the International Meet at Belmont racetrack obviated the immediate need to develop the eastern expanse of the Plains. But flying still remained active at the Mineola field through the summer and fall of 1910, often hosting visiting international aviators and those celebrities shuttling about New York City.

On August 20, 1910, Clifford Harmon flew his Farman biplane from the flying field to Greenwich, Connecticut, for completion of the first flight across Long Island Sound. He departed at 6:35 pm and crash landed at 7:04 pm on the Connecticut shore. Having to alight abruptly, Harmon had no choice but to plow through tall and swaying seagrass:

"I landed on my feet all right and have not even a scratch to remind me of my twenty-eight mile trip. My skids were turned upside down, and the chassis and frame smashed, probably to the extent of $500 damages.

My mechanics will be here tonight, and it will probably take all day tomorrow to take the machine down for shipment to Mineola, where it will be repaired."[13]

On September 16, 1910, Bessica Raiche made the first intentional solo flight by a woman in the United States. Aviation's allure had first drawn Raiche's

Farman biplane, Mineola flying field, 1910.

attention while she was in France. When she moved back to the United States with her French husband, the Raiches set to work upon a pusher biplane in their Mineola home. The Raiches were members of the Aeronautic Society, which had established a service shed at the Mineola Flying Field, and assistance in construction was facilitated by this involvement. Regrettably, Mrs. Raiche's first day of flying ended in a crash. Her fall from thirty feet, however, was not fatal. The daily press reported:

"She scrambled to her feet and before any one of the mechanicians and others who had witnessed the fall of the biplane could reach her, she had shut off the engine and stopped the propeller. She calmly said she was not injured to those who ran to her aid, and then she directed the men to drag the wrecked plane back to the shed."[14]

By summer's end in 1910, as all eyes began to turn towards Belmont Park, Mineola resumed its bustling activity:

"October has brought new life to the place. What with the return of the wanderers from their travels and the hatching of a new nest full of fledglings, the place is busier than ever... Among the new fliers who have been making successful trial flights recently is Henry Charles (Dr.) Cooke... Cooke has a modified Curtiss type machine... On October 8th and 9th he made half a dozen very pretty flights. Either luckier or more skillful than most, he made all of his landings safely, without so much as buckling a wheel or cracking a strut."[15]

Dr. Walden sufficiently recovered from his fall and he was back at Mineola, regaining his feel for the flight controls. He, too, constructed a shed on the corner of the Mineola grounds, in which he tinkered with his designs and began an aircraft manufacturing enterprise.

The charismatic Claude Grahame-White, representing Great Britain in the International Meet, came to Mineola to tune for the imminent competition. He borrowed Harmon's Farman biplane and carried aloft several female passengers who had motored to the field from New York City. Immediately after Grahame-White's low altitude excursions, Tod Shriver, in his Shriver-Dietz biplane, streaked across the field and disappeared in the eastern sky. The New York World reported:

"He turned toward the north shore of Long Island until he reached East Williston. Then he returned to the aviation field, but instead of coming down he continued his flight until he was over Garden City. Then he started back. Nearing the field it took Shriver ten minutes to descend, which he did in one large circle."[16]

In all, Shriver was aloft for 27 minutes and he had attained an altitude of 2,000 feet.

Two days later Prince Tsai Hsun of China toured the Mineola flying field and subsequently viewed the wreckage of Harmon's Farman in a gale:

"A propeller blade was thrown fifty feet in the air and fell with a resounding slap on top of the plane. Harmon's mechanicians carried the machine back in three parts, the engine, the tailpiece, and what remained of the planes. The Prince expressed sorrow at the accident on his account."[17]

Claude Grahame-White easily won the Gordon Bennett Cup at Belmont Park with a winning speed of 61.3 mph. John Moisant of the United States finished second, almost 30 mph behind. Both men were flying Bleriot monoplanes, but Grahame-White's was powered by a 100-hp Gnome, whereas Moisant's rotary only generated 50 hp. After the meet, Moisant continued to tour as an exhibition flier in his troupe of international aviators. On December 31, he was killed while making a practice flight for a competition in New Orleans. Albert Moisant, John's brother, then moved the operation to Long Island and established the foremost flying school and aerodrome of the day. On March 28, 1911, the Hempstead Plains Aviation Company incorporated in Albany, New York:

"As was announced some time ago, when the company was organized, the purposes are to operate and maintain on the Hempstead Plains an aviation school, flying grounds and a factory. Messrs. Moisant and Wupperman are connected with the Moisant International Aviators. Work has already begun toward building hangars and putting the grounds in order for flying."[18]

By this time, Long Island was home to four leading flying fields, each of which was located on the flat Hempstead Plains, though only the grounds of the Moisant School were free from the infringements of streets and village congestion. The environs of Belmont Park to the west were the more densely populated.

The Nassau Boulevard Flying Field at Garden City Estates was the most orderly: grandstands, painted hangars, rolled and sodded field; but the property was in the midst of an affluent suburban community. The Mineola flying field was becoming obsolete and land development was imminent. Finally, the Hempstead Plains, one mile to the east of Mineola, where the Moisants were building the aerodrome, offered the largest uninterrupted tract. The magazine *Aero* reported on April 13, 1912:

"Nassau Boulevard aerodrome is going after all. The occupants of the 31 hangars have received orders to quit before June 1. The entire equipment will be removed to the Moisant Field, one mile to the east of Mineola, thus bringing the ancient flying glory back near to the place where it had its birth on Long Island.

The Moisant Field has an area of 650 acres. There are already several concrete hangars on the ground, and the Moisant company intends building more of the same type, which will be in addition to the wooden sheds that will be removed from Nassau Boulevard.

There is already a high wood fence along the western side of the field. The other three sides are to be marked off with a high wire fence. The majority of the aviators at Nassau Boulevard will probably move to the Moisant field."[19]

The brochure published by the Hempstead Plains Aviation Company described the aerodrome as unique:

"If it is possible to find anywhere a more ideal aerodrome than that of the Moisant Aviation School on the Hempstead Plains at Garden City, certainly the location of that other flying field has not yet been disclosed. When Louis Paulhan, the great French airman, was in the United States early in 1910 he selected the Hempstead Plains Field as indisputably the best whereon to hold last year's International Aviation Tournament. Other leading aviators so thoroughly agreed with the opinion of Paulhan that the committee in charge of the meet decided to hold it at Garden City, to

(Top) Aeronautic(al) Society hangar, Mineola flying field, 1910. (Courtesy Henry Newell)
(Bottom) Moisant Aviation School hangars, Hempstead Plains aviation field, 1912.

move it to Belmont Park a few months later only when it was seen that the limited time at its disposal made it impossible for the committee to erect the necessary buildings and stands on the Hempstead Plains." [20]

With the demise of the Nassau Boulevard Flying Field, the school facilities established by the Moisants were indeed the neatest and trimmest to be found. The Aero Club of America moved its headquarters to the Hempstead Plains Aerodrome in 1912, at which it bestowed the pilot's license, maintained flight records, and sponsored eventful days and special flying tests. A representative of the Aero Club surveyed the field during the summer of 1912:

"The field as it stretches far away in the distance is comparatively level, though halfway out there is a considerable depression in which the school machines disappear from sight when 'grass-cutting'. But this is so gradual that it is quite unnoticed while passing over it. Beyond this bowl is a bluff rising some yards above the lip and forming the edge of another much leveler but extensive field. The runways have been carefully gone over until little is left of the original undergrowth which might entangle the wheels of the chassis, and in time the whole field will be equally smoothed off. The absence of trees, buildings, fences, and water in so large a circuit make of it an ideal field for pupils and pilots to fly over both for tests and exhibitions." [21]

The Moisant School occupied the five steel and concrete hangars on the western border of the field. John Moisant had been a pioneer in the development of the monoplane design, and his brother continued similarly, using monoplanes powered by Anzani or Gnome engines. The School opened in the spring of 1911, before the aerodrome had been completed, so operations emanated from temporary headquarters.

After its premier season in 1911, the Moisant School distinguished itself in a variety of ways: flight instruction as predicated upon consummate knowledge of the aircraft's design and construction; the aircraft were monoplanes rather than the multitudinous adaptations of Wright- and Curtiss-type biplanes; the School initiated classroom techniques for its lectures; and the management welcomed women student pilots.

Harriet Quimby had visited the Belmont Park meet and had become resolute in her desire to learn to fly. She enrolled at the Moisant School in the spring of 1911, and flew throughout the summer. On August 1, 1911, Harriet Quimby became the first licensed woman aviator in the United States, having demonstrated her flying proficiency before judges of the Aero Club.

The second woman in the United States to be officially licensed was Matilde Moisant, sister of the School's director Alfred Moisant. She qualified for her license on August 13, 1911. After the School's first

summer at the emerging aerodrome, fourteen pupils remained enrolled. Chief Instructor was Andre Houpert, one of many international aviators still involved with the Moisant operation even after it settled to permanent quarters after its tours as an exhibition troupe.

The meet at Belmont Park also stimulated Mr. S. S. Jerwan's desire to fly. Jerwan enrolled in the first class of five at the Moisant School in the spring of 1911, and shared student status with Matilde Moisant and Harriet Quimby:

"This school was devoted to the monoplane. When our first class was formed, the flying equipment consisted of one machine (powered by a 25-hp Anzani) built by Moisant along the lines of the Bleriot monoplane. However, this machine could not fly, so it became a primary training machine—that is, a grass-cutter, destined for several years to run back and forth along the ground while students got the feel of various controls." [22]

Jerwan received official license No. 54. As a student, however, he noted many failings in the school's method of instruction and he became determined to eradicate such shortcomings when others sought to fly. He devised slide presentations about flying and animated his discussions with a working model of a monoplane:

"Because of my flying in 1911 and my lectures in the winter of 1911-12, I became fairly well-known, and when the flying season opened in the spring of 1912, Moisant asked me to become chief test pilot and manager of the Moisant School of Aviation. I at once put into effect a system of training which included ground school work, and which called for discipline and conservatism." [23]

Jerwan implored his students to remain cautious at all times. The monoplane used at the Moisant School lacked dual control, so students always had to fly solo. Another difficulty lay in the nearly insignificant difference between top speed and landing speed of the training aircraft. Students were advised to feel their intuitively way about the field. Jerwan's flight training method was a graduated course: students began as grass-cutters, then they continued on to demonstrate control in the straightaway hops, straight flight at 10 feet, circling, turning figure-8s, and finally stunt flying.

"The average student would have only about two hours flying time before taking his license test. This was all solo, of course, for the dual control system was not introduced until later. Obviously, the instructor had a great deal of responsibility and he watched over his students unceasingly. During the three years I was with the Moisant organization, we had only two bad accidents. One pupil got in the way of a machine

(Left) Moisant student Harriet Quimby, first licensed American woman aviator, 1911.

(Below) Moisant Chief Instructor, Andre Houpert, Hempstead Plains, 1911.

which was landing, was hit and died within twelve hours. A total of twenty-seven pilots, representing thirteen countries, were graduated from the school while I was there."[24]

Jerwan continued as the Chief Instructor at the Moisant School through 1913. His pupils included aviators sent from Mexico by the government, and Lieutenant Danti Nanni of the Guatemalan army:

"I was in frequent correspondence with Señor Cabrena, the Dictator-President of that country. As a result of these connections, we sold two Moisant monoplanes to Guatemala and C. Murvin Wood was sent down there to fly for the government and train pilots."[25]

The Moisant School was now firmly ensconced in the five hangars of concrete and steel along the southwest side of the field; and the organization went on to establish a clubhouse which was "fitted up in lavish style for the use of the pupils and other members of the club."[26] Seventeen hangars were occupied by aircraft designers and smaller flight schools, but the activities of the Moisant School were predominant. Jerwan had six monoplanes in daily use while he instructed students in his step-wise fashion:

"George F. Puflea, of Chicago, and William McGinn, of Cincinnati, are two pupils about ready to try for their license; William A. George and Danti Nanni are making straight flights, while two pupils, S. Gordon, of Staten Island, and John McCue, of New York, are grass-cutting and making short hops. . . In addition to the training of pupils there has been considerable flying accomplished at the camp, Harold Kantner having been busy testing the two-seater monoplane for the Guatemala government. . . The new luxurious clubhouse is finding considerable favor with the students and is proving quite an attraction."[27]

(Top) Moisant student and monoplane, Hempstead Plains, 1912.

(Middle) Moisant School monoplane, Hempstead Plains, 1912.

(Bottom) Moisant monoplanes, Hempstead Plains, 1913.

Hangar 30 at the Hempstead Plains Aerodrome was occupied by the brothers Albert and Arthur Heinrich of Baldwin, Long Island. In May, 1910, the Heinrichs earned the distinction of having flown the first American monoplane powered by an American engine, an adapted marine 4-cylinder. The brothers were also taxidermists, experience which inevitably provided an appreciation for the contours of birds' wings— a source exploited in their monoplane designs.

The Heinrichs were the most notable local talent to emerge from the saturation of aeronautical activity on the Hempstead Plains. Initially, they flew from the fields near their home in Baldwin, but with the expansion of the Hempstead Plains aerodrome, commercial opportunities were engendered for the Heinrichs' flight school and aircraft

manufacturing interests. The magazine *Aircraft*, May, 1913, described the Heinrichs as "progressive young men, full of new ideas, and they do not wait for other people to lead the way; they believe in taking the lead themselves and adopting new tactics where those tactics will avail them anything." [28]

The Moisants, Dr. Walden, Walter Fairchild, Frederick Hild — all were instrumental to the introduction of the monoplane in the United States. Fairchild built the first all-metal monoplane and Hild presided over the American Aeroplane Supply Company, in Hempstead, where he manufactured Bleriot-type monoplanes. *Aircraft* noted the latent interest in the monoplanes by U.S. pioneers, and the periodical introduced a new Heinrich design to the public:

"While America is admittedly behind in the manufacture of monoplanes, it is due, we feel sure, through no lack of constructional skill and designing ability on the part of American builders, but rather through the fact that monoplanes have not as yet been accorded the same favor here as abroad.

That our American designers are fully equal to the task is apparent from a study. . . of the monoplane designed by Albert Heinrich, which is undoubtedly the equal in design of any foreign machine so far constructed, and in many respects is considerably an advance of some of the most successful." [29]

The Heinrichs produced new designs throughout the decade and their flight school, like the Moisant, also welcomed women students. Mrs. Mary Sims was taught to fly by Albert Heinrich during 1914, though she never attained her license and subsequently ceased flying after her marriage to her instructor.

The immigrant pioneer Guiseppe Bellanca was another designer who fabricated a monoplane on the Hempstead Plains. He, too, had been drawn to the level Plains from the con-

fines of Morris Park, and his solitary operation subsisted in Hangar 27 at the field. His monoplane was originally powered by an Anzani engine and the craft was remarkable for its diminutive frame.

Ruth Law, the sixth officially licensed woman pilot in the United States, established summer quarters on the Hempstead Plains in August, 1913. After a successful New England tour, Law settled temporarily at the aerodrome with her traveling exhibition company. Before settling on a Curtiss-type, Law pulled her Wright biplane from city to city on a truck hitched to her automobile. She was certainly one of the more promotable women fliers and her flying skills were unmatched. In 1916, she set the men's and women's American nonstop cross-country record when she flew almost 600 miles from Chicago to upstate New York. During World War I Law was the first woman to be authorized to wear a non-commissioned officer's uniform, but her request to fly pursuit in combat was steadfastly denied. [30]

Besides the Moisants and the Heinrichs,

(Top) Frank Fitzsimmons' monoplane, 1911.
(Bottom) Heinrich Model D monoplane, 1911.

(Left) Ruth Law in Curtiss biplane with Wright-type controls, 1913. (Right) Arthur Heinrich and future sister-in-law, Mrs. Mary Sims, in Heinrich monoplane, 1914. (Courtesy Henry Liese)

Frederick C. Hild offered the most services and operated the widest variety of enterprises on the Hempstead Plains. He flew in demonstration flights; he operated a flight school; and he manufactured Bleriot-type monoplanes at the American Aeroplane Supply House, Hempstead, New York, a few miles from the aerodrome.

Hild flew during the four seasons and his operation enabled him both to test the Supply Company's machines and to promote the production aircraft to the public. On July 26, 1913, Hild flew his monoplane in demonstration flights at the Navy Day hosted at the aerodrome. Three thousand persons were in attendance to witness the demonstrated efficacy of the airplane in war.

Sadly, 1913 concluded disastrously for Hild. On December 29, fire ravaged his hangar and destroyed the sheltered aircraft belonging to himself and the Supply Company. *Aero and Hydro*, January 10, 1914, reported that: "The fire raced among the inflammable structures with a speed that made it hard for the men about the place to save any of them. The flames were not checked till they reached the concrete walls of the hangars housing the equipment of the Moisant Aviation School." [31]

Chapter Two

World War I

1917 through 1918

Curtiss 'Jennys,' Hazelhurst Field, 1917.

When war's flames precipitated the U. S. declaration on April 6, 1917, the European Allies were invigorated by the notion that victory was imminent once the industrial might of the United States was waged against the Central Powers. Aeronautical technology in the U. S. lagged behind European aviation in the days before battle, though military aviation was at least comparable amongst the European belligerents who led the aeronautical world previous to 1914. America's seemingly endless natural resources, of course including its labor force, were obviously the enticement to solicit, and expect, unparalleled productive results. The United States felt certain of the same.

By the Armistice of November, 1918, the achievement of American military aviation was prodigious, but its successes were qualified. The development of the high horsepower Liberty engine and the construction of primary training aircraft, mainly the Curtiss JN-4, were sterling marks. The American training program, standardized by May, 1917, was also considered an overwhelming success. The production of European designs by American industry, however, was considered less than adequate, as was the U. S. industry's inability to provide American-designed advanced pursuit ships to the front. In terms of theory, military strategists were divided as to the most efficacious role of the air arm during war.

More than 13,000 Liberty engines were manufactured by November, 1918, and nearly 4,000 Curtiss primary trainers were completed by that time. The U. S. Air Service counted almost 200,000 officers and men at the close of the war, whereas its strength 20 months before numbered merely over 2,000.

The American-produced, British-designed DH-4 was the only foreign design to make it to the front. Communication problems plagued the exchange of essential technical information between Europe and the United States in regard to foreign designs slated to be built in America; and a subsequent preoccupation with policy matters tended to hinder advanced American designs. Many American advanced pursuit ships were obsolete as front fighters by the time they were placed into production. Experienced American designers were also thwarted by a shift in the aircraft industry's growing structure. Large-scale production contracts went to industrialists capable of mass-manufacturing automobiles rather than to pre-war aviation inventors and designers who understood the 'hand-made' nature of airplane production. As far as military strategy was concerned, the U. S. Army was dogmatic in its assertion of a support role for aviation, while the Air Service itself was perceived by its partisans to be an independent force able to provide strategic offense.

World War I was pushed to conclusion by the

revitalizing support of U. S. forces. Had the war continued, the United States would surely have lived up to its production promises of early 1917. During its twenty months involvement in the war, military aviation in the United States matured and fostered trends that would linger prominently throughout the 1920s. When war was declared in 1917, the Army had two officially established flying fields, one of which was located on the site of the Hempstead Plains aviation field and was referred to as 'Mineola.' During the war, the names of the field changed. Though various primary sources indicate a variety of names, the official military designation for the emergent training base was Hazelhurst Field, named after 2nd Lieutenant Leighton Hazelhurst, Jr., who was killed at College Park, Maryland, on June 11, 1912. The eastern portion of the field, the 'Plateau,' became Roosevelt Field after the death of locally trained Quentin Roosevelt, son of President Theodore Roosevelt. Quentin was killed in France at the age of twenty during July 1918. When the military abandoned the northern

(Above) Quentin Roosevelt, 1918.

(Left) Death of Quentin Roosevelt in Nieuport 28, France, July 14, 1918.

(Below) Burial of Quentin Roosevelt, France, July, 1918.

fields for a parcel to the south after the war, this new base became Mitchel Field, named for John Purroy Mitchel, former mayor of New York City and a military flier who fell from a training aircraft also in 1918. Throughout the first several months of war in Europe the still-evolving role of military aviation was assessed, in the United States, more readily by civilians than by the military establishment. When the New York National Guard began its flight training on the Hempstead

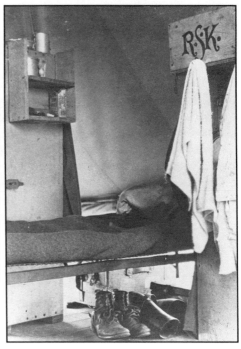

(Top Left) DH-4 wreck, Hazelhurst Field, 1918.
(Top Right) Standard H-3 wreck, Hazelhurst Field, 1918.
(Middle Left) Tent encampment, Hazelhurst Field, 1918.
(Middle Right) Soldier's tent, Hazelhurst Field, 1918.
(Bottom Left) Curtiss 'Jenny,' Hazelhurst Field, 1918.
(Bottom Right) Standard H-3 wreck, Hazelhurst Field, 1918.

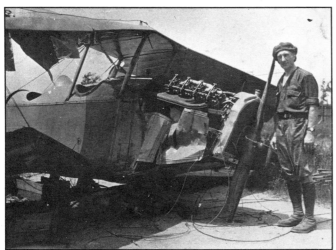

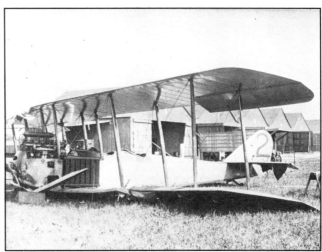

Plains in 1915, it was attracted to the site by virtue of the aeronautical resources present as a result of civil flying activity. Indeed, civilians would continue to fly and train alongside the military through the war period. The Heinrichs had followed the airplane in war through the fall and winter of 1914-15, and by the spring they were demonstrating a rotary-powered tractor biplane on the Plains.

The Heinrichs' 'Military Tractor Biplane' possessed side-by-side seating to facilitate aerial reconnaissance and to allow an exchange of duties between crew members. The lower wing was cut effectively near the fuselage to permit unobstructed ground views and to provide clearance for bomb releases. The undercarriage consisted of a skidded and wheeled landing gear for alighting upon uncertain terrain. In demonstration flights on the Plains, Albert Heinrich carried aloft his wife and then Lieutenant Follett Bradley of the U. S. Army. Heinrich climbed to 2,000 feet and elicited a top speed of 80 m.p.h. from the ship. His landing speed was over 40 m.p.h. In order to meet military specifications, the underside of the craft was lightly armored.

As designers, manufacturers, and flight instructors, the Heinrich brothers were leaders on the Plains. Later, in 1915, the Heinrichs were joined there by the New York National Guard, a unit struggling to coalesce in light of generous but limited civilian support, and in the absence of adequate financial support from the U. S. Government.

Raynal C. Bolling had initiated flight training for himself at Mineola during the summer of 1915. Bolling, a member of the N.Y.N.G., had transferred to the Hempstead Plains from Governor's Island in an attempt to create a prepared and viable air unit. He was joined by several friends and eventually received funds from the Aero Club. The monies were then used to rent Gallaudet tractor biplanes. On November 1, 1915, Bolling took command of the 'Aviation Detachment, First Battalion, Signal Corps, National Guard, New York.'

This First Aero Company enlisted forty men and was led by four officers. By the spring of 1916, the First Aero Company had added five more trainers to its aircraft inventory, four of which were primary tractor biplanes, and one of which was an old Wright pusher. In addition to their flight duty, the men of the First were instructed in aeronautical science and engine maintenance at the Columbia School of Engineering—a method of instruction fully developed in ground schools after April, 1917.

Graham Brush enlisted in the First Aero Company during June, 1916, just previous to the mustering into federal service of the First by the newly arrived Lieutenant Joseph E. Carberry of the regular army. Here Brush describes Mineola as he found it a year after Bolling's arrival:

"At the time there were three hangars, two belonging to the State Guard, the other to the Wright Aeronautical School. There were four (sic) planes on the field that summer, three of our company and the other of the Wright School. It was in this other plane, a 'B' Wright type with two pusher propellers driven by chains from one motor, with the elevators out in front and the seats for pilot and passenger suspended in open air from the frame, that Al Sturtevant learned to fly. . .

The other three planes on the field were old and worn out. Only once during the summer were two of them in operation at the same time. There were about thirty men in the Company and needless to say there was very little flying for any one individual. Our time was spent making camp and repairing the planes, doing a little reading and ground work in spare moments.

There were no buildings at that time on the field, except the hangars, the Company living entirely in tents. It is almost inconceivable that it was only a few years ago when Mineola, the best known field in the country from the very inception of aviation, was nothing more than one of the open spaces of Long Island."[32]

On July 13, 1916, the First Aero Company was mustered into federal service. Skirmishes along the Mexican border and the relative degree of preparedness attained by the First placed the New York National Guard unit in a position of readiness. By the last week of July the Second Aero Company (also from a N.Y. guard unit) arrived at Mineola to continue training alongside the program of the First.

Lieutenant Carberry came to Mineola in July, 1916, with jurisdiction over the First Aero Company, and with the responsibility of developing the Hempstead Plains field into a center of military aviation. When he took command, Carberry found a lack of adequate shelter, support equipment, and repair facilities. Bolling was able to borrow more money from the Aero Club to purchase a training machine and, with difficulty, funds were secured for the application of minimal maintenance upon the aircraft already on the field. Lieutenant Walter Kilner arrived at Mineola during August, 1916, and Carberry assigned to him the task of overseeing flight training. Kilner used the machines of the First Aero Company and the first two government-ordered Curtiss JN-4s. The insufficient appropriation for the support of National Guard flight training led to the abrupt curtailment of the Second Aero Company's training program in September. The need for the First Aero Company along the Mexican border also diminished by late 1916, so the Company was mustered out of federal service on November 2, 1916. Many National Guardsmen, however, remained at Mineola to complete their instruction, though Carberry shifted the emphasis of the station to that of a proving ground. By the end of November, 1916, Mineola counted five officers and forty-eight enlisted men amongst its ranks.

Winter's bite on Long Island quickly illustrated the benefits of flying fields located at warmer latitudes, but at Carberry's insistence, Mineola remained active through the cold months of 1916-17. In fact, Mineola witnessed instructive bomb tests in the course of 1916, and it was Carberry's reasoning that further flight investigations could be made regardless of the weather.

The disbanding of the First Aero Company did not eliminate the National Guard contingent at Mineola. On November 18, 1916, the first National Guard formation flight departed Mineola for Princeton, New Jersey. Over New York Harbor, the seven Mineola 'Jennys' were joined by two others from Governor's Island. On November 20, the return flight was made without incident. A less successful flight occurred on December 30, when a trip composed of Army and National Guard fliers embarked for a frigid ride to Philadelphia. Four of the 12 participating aircraft failed to arrive.

Under Carberry's leadership, the station at Mineola was able to achieve results, much through the desire and resourcefulness of its men. Ground facilities were deplorable. In the roar of winter, many were still living outdoors in tents. A feckless government bid process further slowed the construction of a service building, but by January, 1917, a mess hall, barracks, storehouse, and hospital were completed or at least begun. January 1917 also saw the cessation of flight instruction. Experiments with a metal propeller and with aerial photography underscored the specialty status that Mineola attained at this time. Night flying was explored in detail, with tests in air-to-air and air-to-ground signaling. Formation flights continued through March. On one occasion 25 ships participated in mock reconnaissance maneuvers, and 12 ships flew over the burial site of Peter Millman, a Mineola instructor who came to the field with Bolling's initial charge of Gallaudet tractors. Also, the first aircraft rocketry experiments in the U. S. occurred at Mineola in March, when 'Le Prieur' type rockets were fired from a Jenny. On April 3, 1917, all empirical work ceased at the field and all operations again shifted to flight instruction.

In May 1917, U. S. flight training was standardized. Students were instructed in three phases: ground school, primary flight training, and then advanced pursuit work. Ground schools were established in some of the finer universities, and from there fledgling pilots were sent to a field like Mineola's for primary training. From Mineola, after having successfully passed his military aviator's test, the flight officer proceeded to a larger field for advanced training, perhaps to a field in Texas. Then it was back to Mineola for a fortnight while awaiting embarkation for Europe.

'Jennys' on Hazelhurst Field, 1917.

Hazelhurst Field, 1917.

Stuart Elliot had successfully completed ground school at the Massachusetts Institute of Technology and upon his arrival at Mineola, he was impressed by the rudimentary facilities found there in July, 1917:

"The rest of the post consisted of a few white one-storied barracks, a small headquarters with a flag pole, a water tank, guard house, a few warehouses, and about a half dozen portable, dirt-floored, wooden-framed, wind-ballooning, canvas hangars that housed a motley collection of not very new Jennys, and a few somewhat beat-up looking LWFs... As for the enlisted man's mess hall, it was an open shed adjoining a cook shack, where we placed our mess kits on rough tables, and sat at long benches."[33]

Elliot learned to fly at Mineola in Curtiss JN-4s. The ratings of Military Aviator and Junior Military Aviator were for officers of the regular army who had creditable experience flying. Elliot was restricted to the rating of Reserve Military Aviator, which came after six hours of solo flying. Here he describes the tests for his rating:

"These consisted of a barograph-checked altitude climb to a minimum of twelve thousand feet, which was a long and tedious climb in those primitive Jennys, followed by certain maneuvers to show air proficiency, such as making figure-8s around pylons, and there doing a series of right and then left, tight, vertical spirals, with motor throttled. These over, the candidate had to cut his switch at a minimum altitude of one thousand feet, and land deadstick, to within one hundred feet of a

designated mark. The final test was a cross-country flight to a distant location, a landing at that spot, a take-off, and a return to the field."[34]

Elliot continued on to Texas, where he remained for three weeks. Upon return to Mineola, his class of RMAs was discharged and then commissioned First Lieutenants in the reserve of the Aviation Section, Signal Corps. After the war Elliot returned to Mineola for his official discharge.

The Hughes brothers, Gerard and George, both arrived at Mineola in April, 1917. Gerard had attended ground school at Plattsburg, New York, while George left Harvard a year before his graduation. Both were commissioned 1st Lieutenants in July, 1917, and from there they separated—Gerard to Chanute Field, Rantoul, Illinois, and George to Wilbur Wright Field, Dayton, Ohio. George Hughes returned to Mineola during November, 1917, where he remained until embarking for Europe in December. Gerard Hughes became a flight instructor at Waco, Texas, and did not leave for England until September 8, 1918. After having served overseas, both were honorably discharged on February 5, 1919, on Long Island.

When the Hughes brothers arrived at Mineola in April, 1917, they found it even less hospitable than the base Elliot found three months later:

"When George and I arrived at the old field in April of 1917, the Army was using the five old wood hangars which were along the north side (the Old Country Road side) of the field and also the wooden hangars which had

been built along the Clinton Road—or west side. During our stay at the field, the Army built eight large and up-to-date hangars along the Old Country Road side.

There were fellows from Princeton, Yale, Columbia, Syracuse, Union and, of course, Harvard. Among the latter, I particularly remember John Baker, Duncan Fuller, Roderick Tower (his father had been ambassador to Russia at one time), and Quentin Roosevelt (youngest son of Theodore Roosevelt).

The flying instructors were all civilians who had learned the art in various ways. They were about six in number. The planes were some old Curtiss Jennys that had been kicking about the Signal Corps at various posts. (We did have a French pilot come late as an instructor. He was sent over by France to help us.)

The machine shop and ground crews were put to it to keep enough of the craft in shape to fly so that we could get in the necessary time in the air. The new planes, which were to come later by the thousands, were still to be manufactured.

(For my flight instructor) I drew a young fellow named Wheaton. This lad probably didn't have much more than fifteen total hours in the air when he started with us and was perhaps more afraid of flying than his students. I remember well how he kept a tight grip on the controls all the while I was with him. It was only when he soloed me and I was up there myself that I felt that I was flying the ship.

This experience with Wheaton taught me a lesson because later, when I was instructing, I put myself in the place of my cadets and after a short time with them I held up my hands so that they could see that they were flying—not me!

Only one of our class was killed in training. His name was Carruthers. His instructor was the Frenchman. During a flight lesson they landed the Jenny out on the field and then for some reason or another, Carruthers got out of the plane and went to the front. Probably the motor had stalled and the student was swinging the prop to start it again. Whatever, he accidentally walked or fell into the propeller, was struck on the head and killed.

Each man had had about five or six hours of dual instruction and then, flying solo, we practiced take-offs and landings, over and over again. To this we devoted about ten hours.

Finally we were ready for the RMA tests. First, we had to make a cross-country flight to a point thirty or forty miles distant and back. In our case we flew down the island and landed on a little grassy meadow at Smith's Point.

Next we had to do proper figure-eights. After that it was precision tests seeing if we could land close to a given mark, first with motor running and then with a deadstick. All this business took place over at a great grass-covered stretch of land which lay south of the Plateau.

I think that every member of our class passed the tests and received his RMA rating and his commission as a First Lieutenant (all except Carruthers, of course, since he was killed. . .)

As far as I know, the only member of our original class who got to Europe before George was Quentin Roosevelt—which was not surprising. I think that if our father had been President of the U. S. we would have arrived there early.

Quentin was a nice big good-natured kid. Obviously younger than the rest of us he had probably left the sophomore class at Harvard to join us.

He had his bunk next to mine in the barracks. His bed was one of those regulation canvas folding beds or cots. He found it pretty uncomfortable. I had a good solid steel cot. Quentin complained about his back, saying that he had been thrown by a horse the summer before, out in Wyoming, and would I let him have my nice 'comfy' steel bed? I said 'sure,' as I could sleep well on anything and there was nothing the matter with my back. I am sure that he was telling the truth, and I'm sure glad I did it—under the circumstances."[35]

In November 1917 when George Hughes returned to Mineola to await embarkation for Europe, he wrote a letter to his brother in which he described his squadron's train ride back to New York and the changes made at the field after seven months of war:

"After much telephoning and cussing, a train was made up for us and long about 10:30 p.m. we got underway.

The cars were ice cold when we got into them but by the time we reached Mineola, or rather Garden City, they were well-heated up and we had made arrangements to stay in them all night, so we felt we weren't so

Standard H-3 tractor biplanes, Hazelhurst Field, 1917.

bad off after all.

But when we reached the concentration camp—that is, the old LWF field (later Mitchel Field) the trains ran right out to it over that old electric line that formerly was never used.

We were met by a young Lieutenant who said that a telegram had come from Washington to unload us immediately and quarantine us in barracks just completed but which had no heat, lights or water, and, of course, no cots.

The men had to sleep on the floor under their three little blankets.

About 5:30 a.m. the baggage car with our cook

Curtiss JN-4 ('Canuck' version), Hempstead Plains, 1918.

stoves, grub and cooks came along and I got them backed in on a siding just off the end of barracks #14.

During the day I managed to get cots for every man but could get no heat stoves from the quarter-master of this field—known as Field Two. The old field is now known as Field One.

I went over to Field One today and tried to get a ride. Damn me, you can't get in without a pass, and once in all you can do is turn around and go out again. Won't let you hardly look at a ship. As for getting into one, they act as though they want to put you in the guard house just for the mere asking for a ride.

You need a guide to show the way around. About the only buildings I recognized were the old Wright hangars and the big green ones that were completed before we left.

The new buildings stretch in an unbroken row from the old main entrance to the auto Parkway. In fact, there's about 3 or 4 rows running parallel all the way.

The majority of the ships are the Curtiss As and Ds, with only five or six of the old Bs left—same old tubs that were there in our day and have survived until now. No Standards whatsoever, and only about three LWFs."[36]

The presence of the Curtiss Engineering Corporation at Garden City, contiguous to the south of Hazelhurst Field, was the result of wartime expansion. The massive growth of the Buffalo plant to expedite war contracts alienated the older Curtiss employees who were unused to the mass-production techniques applied to aircraft manufacture, and whose most creative efforts were in design and engineering rather than in production management. This conflict was discerned by the executives administering the Curtiss enterprises during the war, so a split was devised which moved Glenn Curtiss, himself, along with his coterie of favored engineers. Garden City was chosen because of its flying field accessibility and because of the distance between offices on Long Island and in Buffalo. The Curtiss Engineering Corporation continued its experimental design work at Garden City

through the 1920s, and from this factory came one of the postwar's most gratifying projects. Nonetheless, it was wartime production that brought Curtiss back to the Hempstead Plains and it was war's exigencies that led to the construction of aircraft capable of flying across the Atlantic.

The development of the Navy-Curtiss flying boats, the 'NCs', was resultant of the U. S. Navy's desire to find an evasive means of transporting its wartime aircraft to Europe and thereby avoid the menace of patrolling German U-boats which had imperilled crews and car-

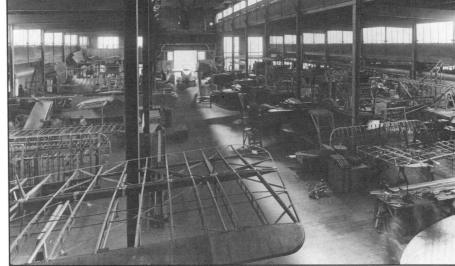

(Right) Curtiss H series flying boats under construction, Garden City, 1918.

(Below) Female employees at Garden City, 1919.

(Left) Construction berth of 'NC-1,' Garden City, 1918.

(Below) 'NC-1,' Garden City, 1918.

goes crossing the Atlantic throughout the war. Glenn Curtiss was initially hired as a consultant to the project, and though the Navy obviously supported the program, the service wished to allow development without diminishing projects already established as priorities. In an effort to keep its own production facilities unimpeded during the 'NCs' creation, a production contract was made with the Curtiss Engineering Corporation on January 8, 1918. Design work continued at Buffalo on the flying boats until December, 1917.

Then, after the Navy expanded floor space at Garden City to accommodate the new ships, the project was moved by train to Long Island. The Naval Air Station at Rockaway was also expanded to house the 'NCs', and it was from this station that the ships began their flights.

The 'NC-1', initially powered by three Liberty engines, was the only ship constructed before the end of the war. However, the U. S. Navy wished the laurels of having successfully completed the first trans-Atlantic flight, so the project continued apace with this goal as its objective. The 'NC-1' was the only ship in the class to have its hull built by Curtiss; the other three hulls were constructed by boat builders under contract. In all, four 'NCs' were built for the trans-Atlantic flight but the

NC-2 was wrecked and cannibalized for parts before the flight began. The flight plan called for departing North America at Trepassy Bay, Newfoundland, to alight at the Azores, and then continue to England via Portugal. The 'NC-3' alighted at sea, shy of the Azores, and was subsequently steered like a boat on the sea to port. The 'NC-1' never made the Azores and its crew was forced to abandon ship. The crew was secured and the 'NC-1' sunk to keep clear the shipping lanes. The 'NC-4' arrived at the Azores on May 17, 1919, continuing on to Lisbon and then Plymouth, England, where it was jubilantly received on May 31. Though three of the four 'NCs' never made it across the Atlantic by virtue of their wings, the 'NC-4' and its crew were toasted the world

(Above) LWF V-1, Hazelhurst Field, 1918.

(Right) LWF 'Shark,' Hazelhurst Field, 1918.

(Below) LWF 'Owl,' Roosevelt Field, 1920.

over as first across what seemingly had been an impenetrable natural barrier.

Along with the production of the Model F and H series flying boats at the Engineering Corporation, Curtiss also developed experimental pursuit ships and produced the two-seat 'Dunkirk' fighter. Another Curtiss design, the HS 2L flying boat, was contracted to the LWF Engineering Company at College Point, Long Island. LWF had been organized in 1915 by Edward Lowe, Jr., Charles Willard, and Robert Fowler. Willard, chief designer at LWF, had been the first Curtiss student at Mineola in 1909. The company derived its acronym from the surnames of the founders, but after the sale of the company, the letters were retained in deference to the popular conception of its derivation from the company's most significant design attribute, the laminated wood fuselage.

The Model V of 1916, a training biplane, initiated LWF's successful endeavors, and the ship was remarkable for its durability at the hands of student pilots. In 1917, the Model G two-place, Liberty-powered biplane appeared, and though its production was stymied by the official pursuance of the DH-4 design, the G was a finely crafted airplane. For the postwar market, LWF busied itself with the colossal Model H for potential mail routes. The giant 'Owl,' powered by three Liberty engines, interested the government as a mail carrier or a bomber, though costs prohibited manufacturing more than one. First flights were made at Hazelhurst Field during 1920.

The most notable foreign aircraft to be found about Hazelhurst Field during 1918 were the Caproni bombers, Italian aircraft whose American production was marred by obfuscated contracts, inappropriate technical conversions, and language barriers. The first American-made bomber flew over Hazelhurst Field, on July 4, 1918, and an Italian contingent was stationed at the field to instruct U. S. pilots. SVA fighters were also delivered to Hazelhurst, where they remained after the Armistice. The Caproni biplane 'Julius Caesar' was based at the field and it participated in the New York-Toronto race in August, 1919.

Finally, mention should be made of the Air Service Medical Research Laboratory which was established at Hazelhurst on January 19, 1918, initially for expediting pilot selection but eventually for testing those already trained to fly. A rebreathing machine was devised which enabled simulation to determine a pilot's response to oxygen deprivation at increasing altitudes. With the initiation of flight surgeons' training in May, 1919, the laboratory was moved to Mitchel Field where it remained until 1926.

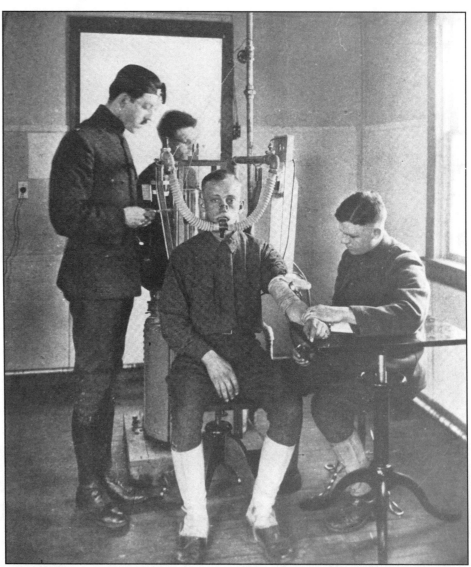

Rebreathing apparatus, Air Service Medical Research Laboratory, 1918.

Chapter Three

The Decade of Great Flights
1919 through 1927

Flying Festival, Curtiss Field, 1921.   AVIATION HERITAGE

1919 through 1920

During the 1920s, aviation grew and spread its reach through all aspects of American life and culture. The war had created an industry in a conspicuously brief span of months and men by the thousands had been taught to fly. Though most persons remained skeptical of the airplane's promise in peacetime, there had developed in the minds of some a vision of the airplane's unprecedented potential. The Air Corps Act of 1926 achieved for military fliers a more distinct organization which relied increasingly upon its own operational independence. The military pioneered regular airmail service and it sponsored races and flights of pure speed and of fabulous duration. Billy Mitchell blasted his way to court-martial while exposing weaknesses in traditional military thinking so far as it applied to the airplane; and naval aviation achieved character of its own with the addition of the aircraft carrier to the twentieth-century's arsenal.

Commercially, the most difficult obstacle for the struggling aviation industry was the lack of a strong market for its product—whether for business flying or pleasure—and this in face of inexpensive surplus air-craft both from home and from abroad. Aviation's incomplete infra-structure made it difficult for the general public to visualize the accessibility and convenience promised by swarms of airplanes servicing commerce and delivering passengers. The veritable unreliability of engines and aircraft was enough to quell mass conversion to the air age.

Nonetheless, the 1920s were the remarkable years within which aviation built its base and forged the frame necessary for the blossoming of the airplane's 'Golden Age' on Roosevelt Field's runways in the 1930s. The military moved to the south and developed Mitchel Field into a thriving center of military aviation. Military fliers would use Hazelhurst/Curtiss Field as the eastern terminal of the transcontinental mail route until 1925 and above Roosevelt and Mitchel Fields, the skies were torn by the fastest military pursuits of the day.

The Hempstead Plains were also home to the most professional engineering and manufacturing firm of the 1920s. The Curtiss Company, in its scope and breadth, was unique. In some classes, its aircraft had no peers. Its engineering and design work attempted to be progressive—and this in light of a depressed commercial market. Its flying services offered to the public all means and methods to stimulate interest in airplanes—from the financing of a personal ship to a short sight-seeing trip over local villages. Curtiss and Roosevelt Fields' exciting activity was a magnet, and to the fields were drawn aviation's illustrious personalities.

Finally, within the decade following the Armistice, and having the charge to ignite in the general public an awareness of a future world linked by invisible routes through the air, were the magnificent flights by the magnificent, provocative pilots themselves, men and women who strove to be the fastest or highest or farthest flown from amongst all who had ever dwelt upon the earth.

Perhaps nothing in the history of Roosevelt Field presented a more glorious sight than the moored H.M.A. R-34 in the summer sun of 1919. On the morning of July 6, the R-34 made visual contact with the New England coast:

"July 6th 4 am — Sighted the American coast at Chatham. Half an hour later Major E. H. Scott is wondering whether petrol will allow him to go to New York or if it would not be more prudent to land at Montauk Point.

5:30 am — Passing over Martha's Vineyard, a lovely island and beautifully wooded. Scott decides that he could just get through to Hazelhurst Field but not enough fuel to fly over New York. Very sad but no alternative. We will fly over New York on our trip back, weather permitting. Landed 1:45 pm Greenwich time, or 9:45 am U.S.A. time at Hazelhurst Field (sic), Long Island.

Total time entire voyage—108 hours, 12 minutes." [37]

After having departed East Fortune, Scotland, on July 2, 1919, the R-34 made its lengthy westward voyage without mishap, though it had fought severe weather conditions causing its fuel supply to be nearly exhausted upon making Mineola. The possibility of the ship being unable to reach Roosevelt Field was apparent to the officers and men who composed the airship's awaiting ground crew, so a contingent left the field by automobile to travel to Montauk to afford assistance there. While heading east, the R-34 was passing

westward overhead of the entourage, so the men on the ground reversed direction to meet the ship back at Roosevelt. The *Air Scout* of July 15 reported:

"Rumor after rumor of disaster and near disaster came in and it seemed for a while as if it would be necessary to send out ships to hunt for the missing airship. Just as all hope of the success had faded word was received of her passage over Montauk and shortly afterward the aerial monster was seen in the far distance over Westbury and it slowly circled the field twice.

After the second 'tour de piste' the engines were stopped and a black object was detached from the forward car and rapidly fell earthward. After a short descent it suddenly transformed itself into a man carrying a parachute. It was Major Pritchard who had decided to take this method of landing in order to superintend the berthing of the R-34.

Shortly after Major Pritchard had landed the big ship dipped her nose toward the berthing space marked out by hydrogen flasks and descended with the wind, contrary to the usual method of landing aircraft, until the eager outstretched hands of the landing party could

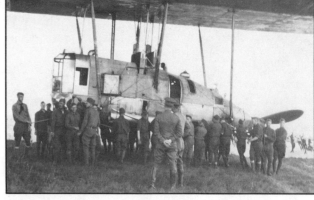

(Top) Moored R-34, Roosevelt Field, 1919.

(Bottom) Gondola of R-34, Roosevelt Field, 1919.

H.M.A. R-34, Roosevelt Field, 1919.

grasp one of the mooring cables thrown out by the ship's crew." [38]

Major E. H. Scott, commander of the R-34, and his crew were hosted by the officers of Mitchel Field later that night. Scott applauded the efforts of his American ground crew:

"Kindly convey to all those who were responsible for the excellent handling of the the H.M.A. R-34 during her stay at Hazelhurst Field (sic), Long Island, my sincerest thanks and gratitude.

The care given the R-34 could not have been bettered by the crew of East Fortune. In fact this is the first time a ship of this kind has been moored in the open and there was no precedent. American ingenuity made possible the safety of the ship. I hope to have the pleasure of visiting America in the near future with a larger and better ship than the R-34 and I can assure you that I will have no fear for the safety of it while it is in charge of such crews as handled the R-34 during its visit." [39]

Visitors streamed to the field during the course of the R-34's four day stay. Even Brigadier General Billy Mitchell came to inspect the rigid airship before its departure on the night of July 9. Preston Bassett, a searchlight engineer for Sperry, also visited the field the night the R-34 departed for Europe:

"I got to bed a little before 3 am this morning after helping the R-34 start for England. The early part of the evening I spent out at the aviation field where the R-34 was tugging at her ropes in a stiff breeze, and stretching and pulling her 500-man anchors around with her. . . The whole big scene with the five or six hundred men all working around under the big gas bag, as large as the Woolworth Building lying on its side, was all illuminated in a bright flood of light from our open-type lights. Men were running around with gas tanks, pulling and hauling on ropes, and in general making the last preparations. I had no trouble getting through the guards who were keeping spectators about 2 1/4 miles away; and once through, I found my way to headquarters and invited myself in, found the crew of the R-34 all dressed in their flying togs ready to start and just sort of waiting around. They were the coolest, least excited bunch of men on the whole field, and calmly talking to reporters and taking their last smokes. . . I found them ready to talk and got acquainted with a few of them, saw Commander Scott and made arrangements with him about throwing our searchlights on him from the Sperry Building so that New Yorkers could see the ship." [40]

By midnight, Bassett was back in Brooklyn playing his lights upon the R-34 as it began its safe passage eastward across the Atlantic.

The Reliability Tours of the mid 1920s went far to promote the cause of aviation. No tours were more successful than those undertaken by the 'Spirit of St. Louis' in 1927-28. These flights were scheduled in advance, and therefore, when pilot and ship dropped from the sky as expected, were meaningful indicators to the public of the airplane's increasing reliability. In 1919, however, the organized races and tours were more accurately displays of technical insufficiency in comparison to the type of equipment actually needed to cover vast and topographically varied distances.

Departing both from Roosevelt Field and from Toronto during August, 1919, to embellish the conclusion of Canada's National Exhibition, 52 entries attempted to conquer the 1,042 miles between terminals. More than half the aircraft participating were war surplus though the event's sponsoring organization stated its aims as a promotion of "the science and sport of aviation in a manner reflecting its safety, reliability, and permanence." Twenty-eight airplanes finished.[41]

The second race occurred between October 8 and 31. 'The Great Transcontinental Reliability and Endurance Test' was more realistically perceived by its organizers as a demonstration of the woeful state of contemporaneous aircraft. Its intentions were also more immediate in the sense that Billy Mitchell and the Post Office were insistent upon proving the feasibility of the transcontinental mail.

"October 8 dawned clear and cool with a fresh northeasterly wind. More than 2000 spectators showed up at Roosevelt Field, Long Island, for the day's festivities. The 22nd Infantry Band provided music, while ladies from the War Camp Community Service passed out sandwiches and coffee to contestants and guests. Assistant Secretary of War Benedict Corwell, a supporter of unification, was on hand. Billy Mitchell arrived from Washington, where he had been testifying in support of a separate air force before House and Senate committees."[42]

The first day of the race ended with five crashes and a death toll of three. In all, seven fatalities were counted. Lieutenant Belvin W. Maynard won the race piloting a DH-4. He landed at Roosevelt Field on October 18 after having flown to San Francisco via Buffalo, Cleveland, Chicago, Omaha, Cheyenne, Salt Lake City, Reno, and Sacramento—and then back again to New York. Only eight contestants completed the round-trip. The accidents had been ferocious

during the race and few adherents to the idea of a transcontinental mail route were won.

Airmail operations had been associated with the Hempstead Plains since September, 1911, when Earle Ovington flew over the Mineola Flying Field and dropped a sack of mail. In May, 1918, regular airmail service was begun from the New York terminal located at Belmont Park. Heller Field in Newark, New Jersey, replaced Belmont Park as the terminal for the New York-Washington route in 1919, but Hazelhurst Field was leased by the Post Office to serve as the eastern terminal of the transcontinental mail.

The equivocal results of Mitchell's endurance and reliability race left undiminished the desire on the part of some to initiate the transcontinental mail. Besides needed ground services across the country, the Post Office was in continuous search for better aircraft for its flight routes. Modification of DH-4s by LWF at College Point, Long Island, and the introduction of the JL-6 all-metal monoplane pointed to alternatives for mail carriage, but subsequent fatalities and structural defects grounded these aircraft from replacing the regular DH-4s then in service. On September 8, 1920, the transcontinental mail departed Hazelhurst Field in a DH-4. On September 11, the mail made San Francisco after having traversed the continent in nearly 83 hours. On February 22, 1921, the mail departed San Francisco in a DH-4 headed east. Almost 34 hours later, Ernest Allan landed at Hazelhurst Field (Curtiss Field), by which the first demonstration of transcontinental day and night service was completed. Regular day and night service began in July, 1924. By December, the transcontinental terminal on Long Island was moved to

Airmail hangar and Curtiss 'Night Mail' conversion, Curtiss Field, 1922.

Hadley Field in New Brunswick, New Jersey, in an effort to streamline operations.

Though the early postwar years limited the demand, and therefore the production of new aircraft designs, some wartime experimental craft were progressive enough to distinguish themselves after the Armistice. For the war, Curtiss developed the 18-T triplane at Garden City. The 18-T 'Wasp' set an unofficial speed record of 163 miles per hour in 1918. The U. S. Navy requisitioned the construction of two 18-Ts from Curtiss, but the war's cessation obviated the service's need for both ships. The 18-T-2 remained at Garden City for further testing and was subsequently flown by Curtiss test pilot Roland Rholfs when he established the new world's altitude record of 34,910 feet over Roosevelt Field on September 18, 1919. Rholfs had moved to Garden City from Buffalo to become chief test pilot for Curtiss in 1917. Previous to his altitude record he had flown in the New York-Toronto race in August.

Immediate postwar designs constructed by Curtiss to exploit the optimistically foreseen aviation boom included the 'Oriole' and the 'Eagle', the first Curtiss aircraft to utilize birds names for their designations. Both craft were flown in 1919 by another Curtiss test pilot who had arrived at Garden City during the war. Bert Acosta would be a fixture at Curtiss and Roosevelt Fields throughout the 1920s, stunting in an old Curtiss pusher, demonstrating Curtiss racers for the military, and eventually become a crew member in one of 1927's great flights.

The successful production and subsequent poor sales of the 'Oriole' epitomized the problems faced by Curtiss in the years following the war. Its design was a detailed advance over wartime airplanes, but prices had to be slashed in half several years later to clear factory space:

"The 'Oriole' was still a significant design . . . Its seating arrangement, pilot in the rear cockpit and two passengers sitting side by side in the front, with their entrance enhanced by anchoring the center section struts ahead of the cockpit and adding a small door at the side, became the standard for practically all American three-seat biplanes built up to the mid-1930s."[43]

Originally powered by new war surplus OX-5 engines, the 'Orioles' eventually used upgraded Curtiss K-6 and C-6 engines. Casey Jones, manager of the Curtiss Flying Service through the 1920s, flew an OX-5 to a handicapped first place finish in the 1923 *On to St. Louis Race.* In 1924, with the wings of his 'Oriole' clipped and the powerplant improved to a C-6, Jones again won first place, this time in the *On to Dayton Race.* The Ireland 'Comet' was a clipped-wing 'Oriole' that G. S. Ireland produced from his small plant established near the Curtiss factory in Garden City. Cheap surplus aircraft were vanishing by 1925, so Ireland attempted to undercut the new airplane market with his inexpensive adaptations of the 'Oriole.'

Curtiss built three versions of the Eagle—one, two, and three-engined models. Bearing structural similarities to the 'Oriole,' the 'Eagle' was envisioned as an airliner capable of carrying crew, passengers,

WILLIAM WAIT

Curtiss Eagle, proposed Inter-City Airliner on Curtiss Field, 1920. This is a tri-motor Eagle and versions were also built with one or two engines.

Casey Jones and his "Clipped Wing" Oriole on Curtiss Field in the early 1920s. Jones won many races with this, his personal aircraft.   WILLIAM WAIT

and freight. The 'Eagle' made its first public flights on September 27, 1919. On October 24, the 'Eagle' departed Garden City for a flight to Washington, D. C., via Phildelphia:

> *"The recent flight, on which I was privileged to be a passenger, of the Curtiss 'Eagle' from Roosevelt Field to Philadelphia has convinced me that the chief responsibility for the development of the aeroplane as a commercial factor has passed from the designers and builders to the public.*
> *In fact, so far as I can see, the only stumbling block in the path of further commercial development of the aeroplane is the prejudice on the part of the public, and incidently, the government. . . "*[44]

In 1920, Acosta test flew the single-engined 'Eagle' over Curtiss Field with a useful load of 3,533 pounds. Again, a Curtiss design presaged later aeronautical innovation but, as before, the demand for the ship was minimal:

> *"This machine is adapted to either passenger or freight carrying. Entrance is made through a side door reached by means of disappearing steps. The enclosed cabin compartment is finished in leather with eight individual upholstered seats, staggered to permit easy movability, dome lights, curtained windows of celluloid and triplex, giving protection from wind and noise, and at the same time free vision."*[45]

In the immediate postwar period, Curtiss retained only two of its factory plants; Buffalo and the Engineering Corporation at Garden City. By 1920, the pitiful civilian aviation market forced Curtiss from commercial production and all contracts through 1925 represented military work. In the reorganization of 1920, Clement Keys became president of the Curtiss Aeroplane and Motor Company, and Glenn Curtiss returned to active management.

> *"The reorganization of the Curtiss Company was also marked by the purchase from the government of Hazelhurst Field adjacent to the Curtiss plant at Garden City. The company's policy is to make this new Curtiss Field available as far as possible to the general public. The Aero Club of America has accepted the offer of club headquarters and hangar space at the field."*[46]

Two aircraft types constructed at the Garden City plant, but not Curtiss designs, were the Orenco D single-seat biplane fighter and the Martin MB-2 bomber. The designs of both were owned by the government which offered contracts by bid to manufacturers other than the original designers. In this way, more postwar manufacturers were able to maintain minimal production levels even though they were without original design contracts.

The Curtiss Flying Service moved to permanent Garden City headquarters with the purchase of Curtiss Field in 1920. In the next ten years every aspect of civil and commercial flying was offered to the public — flight training, emergency air transport, sight-seeing tours. In ten years it was estimated that 50,000 passengers had flown over 500,000 miles from the Curtiss Field terminal. The Curtiss company made good its promise to keep available Curtiss Field.

WILLIAM WAIT

(Top Left) *Curtiss Model CT Torpedoplane, one completed at Garden City, 1921.*

(Top Right) *Italian Ansaldo SVA, Hazelhurst Field, 1918.*

(Above) *Students and instructors of Curtiss Flying Service, Curtiss Field, 1921.*

(Right) *Curtiss 18-T triplane, 1919. Flown by Roland Rholfs to set new world's altitude record of 34,910 feet.*

(Below) *Curtiss-built Martin MB-2 bomber, Curtiss Field, 1924.*

(Above) Students and instructors of Curtiss Flying Service, Curtiss Field, 1921.

(Below) Handley-Page bomber, Roosevelt Field, 1920.

1921 through 1925
Aviation Day, October 1921 -- Curtiss Field

Flying Festival, Curtiss Field, 1921.

"The Contest Committee of the Aero Club of America announces that Aviation Day will take place on the Curtiss Field at Mineola on Sunday, October 16, through the courtesy and cooperation of the Curtiss Company in lending the field.

There will be keen competition between the manufacturers. By having the exhibits on the field instead of in buildings the public may examine them at their leisure without being afraid of missing any flying. Each exhibitor is requested to make one or more exhibition flights to show the performance of his plane, motor, etc. The nature and duration of each flight should be sent in writing to the Contest Committee of the Aero Club. In this way anyone interested in a plane will know what time it will fly, and furthermore the public will know at all times what planes are in the air." [47]

By 1925, the Curtiss Company and its subsidiary flying service at Garden City were buttressing the aviation industry in more ways than any other institution:

"Sixty students were taught to fly and a large percentage passed the FAI test given by the National Aeronautic Association. Most of the nearly 4,000 passengers were carried on the popular $5 hops of ten miles. In the aerial photographic field the company does no actual photography but furnishes the flying service for all the large aerial photographic companies." [48]

When in 1927, Roosevelt Field, in shouting distance to the east, was feverish with trans-Atlantic preparations, the pace of contiguous Curtiss Field literally doubled:

"During the year the Curtiss Flying Service carried slightly more than ten thousand passengers, an increase of more than 100% over the number carried in 1926. Students enrolled during 1927 numbered 310 and of these 224 soloed, as compared to 95 in 1926." [49]

The superb facilities of the Engineering Corporation at Garden City included a specially housed wind tunnel (which at the time was the only wind tunnel in the United States owned by an airplane manufacturing enterprise), and a precision model shop. The wind tunnel's airstream was generated by a 12-foot propeller and a 400 hp motor. From this sophisticated environment emerged Garden City's most dashing ships of the 1920s, the Curtiss Racers.

The instigation for designing and constructing racing aircraft at Garden City came at the request of a civilian who wished to enter the Gorden Bennett races in 1920. The two racers, the 'Texas Wildcat' and the

Aircraft of Curtiss Flying Service and Exhibition Company, Curtiss Field, 1921.

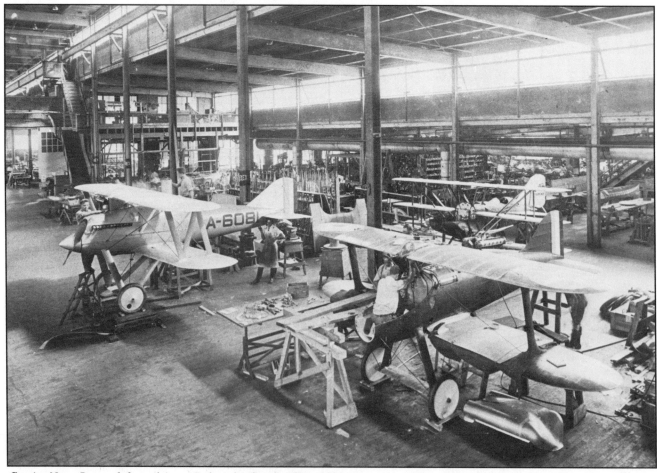

Curtiss Navy Racer, left, and Army R-6, right, Garden City, 1922.

'Cactus Kitten,' were built for S. E. J. Cox of Texas, and thus the ships were dubbed the Cox racers. The 'Texas Wildcat' was wrecked in France before the race, and the 'Kitten' was subsequently re-appointed with triplane wings. It finished second in the 1921 Pulitzer race before becoming the U. S. Navy's triplane trainer.

From the design of the Cox racers came the Model 23, the Navy Curtiss Racer and the Army R-6. The U. S. Navy withdrew from the 1921 Pulitzer race, but Curtiss was able to borrow the ship as its own entry. Piloted to a first place finish by Bert Acosta, the CR-2 won the Pulitzer Trophy with a speed of 176.1 mph. This same CR-2, Navy-designed A6081, was flown to a third place finish by Lt. H. J. Brow in the 1922 Pulitzer. In 1923, the racer was converted to a seaplane in which configuration it finished first in the Schneider Trophy race.

In 1923, the U. S. Navy ordered two new Curtiss racers, designed R2C-1s, for the October Pulitzer contest. Lt. Alford J. Williams flew Navy designated A6692 to the first place in 243.68 mph; second was won by Lt. Brow in A6691, 241.77 mph. Brow's racer was put on floats and entered in the 1924 Schneider Trophy race, which was cancelled. A6691 then served as a trainer until wrecked in 1926.

Scrambling for more military work in the midst of its wildly successful racing series, Curtiss embarked upon the construction of a single-seat biplane fighter:

"In mid-January 1923, the first PW-8 (Curtiss model 33, design L-18-1), was rolled out on the snow-covered field at Garden City, Long Island. This airplane had not been developed to any government specifications, but was a proprietary design developed privately by Curtiss at their own expense."[50]

From the PW-8 (pursuit, water-cooled) was refined the P-1 series, the first production models in the Curtiss 'Hawk' line, which continued production variations until 1938. In all, over 700 'Hawks' were built by Curtiss—some in Garden City, most in Buffalo.

Of final note was the development in 1921 of an all-metal propeller by Dr. Sylvanus Reed at the Engineering Corporation at Garden City. It was known as the Curtiss-Reed propeller due to the sponsorship of the Curtiss company:

"Increased efficiency over the wooden propeller, freedom from warping and deterioration under any climatic conditions, absolute indestructibility by hail, rain, high grass, etc., smoothness, and freedom

Navy Curtiss CR-2, A6081, and Lt. H. J. Brow, Curtiss Field, 1922.

Navy Curtiss CR-2, 1921 Pulitzer winner, piloted by Bert Acosta, 1921.

Navy Curtiss R2C-1, A6691, 1922 Pulitzer second place winner, piloted by Lt. H. J. Brow, 1923.

Navy Curtiss triplane trainer, Curtiss Field, 1923.

Curtiss-Reed all-metal propeller, 1924.

from vibration have made it indispensable to air navigation."[51]

Curtiss-Reed propellers remained in production from 1923 until World War II.

The imaginative variety of uses to which the airplane was put in the 1920s included aerial photography, crop-dusting, forest patrols, surveying, ambulance medical service, and the decidedly commercial means of scripting messages in the sky. The *Aircraft Yearbook of 1924* wrote: "Aerial advertising came into great prominence during 1923, when the Skywriting Corporation of America introduced this new and spectacular use of the airplane to this country."[52] The Skywriters operated from Curtiss Field, at which it based part of its fleet of SE-5s, surplus British designs produced in the United States during the war. The corporation promoted itself by pointing to its maintenance of pursuit ships as providing a benefit to the nation in case of international strife or disaster:

"The type of airplane used for Skywriting is actually a fighting airplane—a type known in army circles as a high altitude pursuit ship. Our pilots when Skywriting can perform the same maneuvers used in air fighting. A Skywriting ship can be turned into a fighting ship at a few hours notice. . . Skywriting is perhaps the only section of the advertising profession which is of direct military value to the Nation."[53]

The Skywriters served more than their clients. An estimated fifty million persons were exposed to the airplane in the course of the Skywriters' first year in the United States, and the fleet of aircraft flew over a quarter million miles. Louis Meier was a pilot for the Skywriting Corporation at Curtiss Field. In 1924 he was asked to fly in mock combat for the feature *Skyraiders,* the

Director (pointing), Charles Nungesser (second from right), and Louis Meier (right) during filming of "Skyraiders," Roosevelt Field, 1924.

Cast and crew of "Skyraiders," Roosevelt Field.

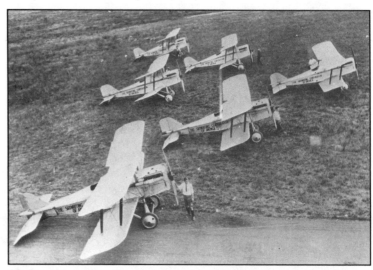

SE-5s of Skywriting Corporation of America, Curtiss Field, 1923.

Skywriting Corporation of America personnel, Curtiss Field, 1923.

Skywriting over Long Island, circa 1923.

SE-5s of Skywriting Corporation of America, Curtiss Field, 1923.

first aviation film made on Roosevelt Field, and it starred French ace Charles Nungesser. In the scene Meier was to succomb to Nungesser's guns:

"You know, it was the damndest thing. I don't know what came over me. I knew I was supposed to circle around and let him shoot me down, but when I came barreling out of a dense cloud cover, there he was—one of the world's greatest combat pilots—square in my gunsights! It was the chance of a lifetime and I couldn't bring myself to waste it. So, with all those fake bullets in my guns, I shot the great French ace out of the sky, side-slipped into a landing, jumped out of the ship, and ran like hell! I knew the director would fire me. He'd have to, for, of course, Nungesser was mad.

When I started to laugh, it struck him so funny that he roared right along with me. The whole thing wound up by my being hired back again, and we went up and did the

Sikorsky S-29A, twin-engine transport, in flight over Long Island, 1925.

Parachutists board S-37, Roosevelt Field, 1927.

whole thing over the way it should have been done in the first place."[54]

Nungesser's presence and the commotion wrought by the film crew drew to the field many reporters who were covering stories for their papers. Unwittingly, the large crowd was subsidizing the efforts of an immigrant Russian who was hardly well-established, and who was struggling to keep vital his small manufacturing team. Igor Sikorsky's S-29A twin-engined transport had just crashed on a golf course next to the field, and prospects

Repaired Sikorsky S-29 disguised as a German bomber for aviation film, "Hell's Angels," 1926.

Sikorsky S-37, Roosevelt Field, 1927.

of future financial support were unpromising. Indeed, he took what he could:

"Captain Nungesser, the French ace, had come to Roosevelt Field to give exhibitions, and the newspapers were much interested in him, as we were ourselves. By some miracle, the telephone bill had been paid for two months in advance, and as it was the only telephone at our end of the field newspapermen used it frequently. They paid for their calls, and at the end of the day we would grab a dollar change, or perhaps more, and go out to buy milk and bread for our lunch or dinner."[55]

Sikorsky always credited the dedication of his workers for his success. On the brink of ruination after the wreck of the S-29A, Sikorsky was able to rally his men for one last subscription, by which he wished to salvage the S-29. With two overhauled Liberty engines the plane flew again:

"The ship was probably the first, or at least one of the first, twin-engined airplanes built in the United States capable of flying on one motor. It had a large passenger cabin which would hold fourteen passengers; a maximum speed of 115 miles an hour. It had good take off and landing characteristics,

Burnelli RB-1, 1921.

and in spite of the difficulties experienced during its construction, it proved to be a very strong machine."[56]

The S-29 was sold in 1926, and it met its fate in flames when disguised as a German bomber for an aviation film. It was set ablaze while aloft. Also in 1926, Sikorsky continued work on the S-34 twin-engined amphibion and on the S-37, the latter having interested Rene Fonck as a potential 1927 trans-Atlantic transport. Hangar space was rented at Roosevelt Field and factory space was utilized in College Point. By 1928, the Sikorsky Manufacturing Corporation reorganized to better handle increased business due to its successful twin-engined, ten-seat amphibion, S-38. By 1929, Sikorsky had established new quarters in Connecticut.

One of the stranger aircraft to fly about Curtiss and Roosevelt Fields was the Burnelli RB-1 biplane with a fuselage designed to assist the wings in generating lift. Vincent Burnelli established a manufacturing plant in Amityville, Long Island, in 1920. In August, 1924, the RB-2 was test flown at Curtiss Field, attaining an altitude of 4200 feet. The RB-2 flew freight for eight years before being scrapped.

Nothing in the 1920s did more to generate excitement and support for aviation than the great flights. In some instances these flights were sponsored by the military; others were races or endurance tests. To achieve these flight goals, courage, stamina, and skill were demanded of the pilots. As for the required aircraft, airframes and engines were able to endure the seemingly limitless hours and incredible distances to be covered.

On December 29, 1921, Lloyd Bertaud and Eddie Stinson took off from Roosevelt Field at 8:58 am in a Junkers-Larsen JL-6 monoplane powered by a 185 hp BMW engine. When they landed at 11:17 am on the 30th, they had successfully completed the longest en-

durance flight since June, 1920, when a Farman 'Goliath' remained in the air over 24 hours.

Gale winds blew continuously through the night of the 29th while the temperature dropped to zero degrees. To aid the pilots, a lighted arrow was marked on the field pointing to the north. Members of the Aero Club alternated as observers throughout the flight, and it was reported that:

". . . although the plane was invisible during the night, the hum of the motor was continuously heard. At times the machine was discernible by the occasional flares from the exhaust as a dark shade moved by directly overhead."[57]

Although the pilots contended that the monoplane could have lasted five more hours with the fuel on board, oil trouble forced them to alight after breaking the previously held endurance record by two hours.

The first nonstop transcontinental flight in the United States departed Roosevelt Field on May 2, 1923 and landed in San Diego on May 3, after flying 26 hours, 50 minutes. The aircraft, a Fokker F-IV named 'T-2,' was piloted by Lieutenants Oakley Kelly and John MacCready of the U. S. Air Service. The Roosevelt Field take-off was the third attempt at the transcontinental record, but it was the only attempt in an east-west direction.

The 'T-2' was to take off east to west across the field in accordance with the normal westerly winds, but the wind shifted so the 'T-2' redressed accordingly. On its first take-off run the power was cut because Kelly felt uncertain of clearing electric wires and trees bordering the field. In the second attempt, this time made from the southeast of Roosevelt towards the northwest of Curtiss, the 'T-2' was still earthbound as it approached the edge of the 'Plateau':

"The big monoplane bounced and bounced but did not rise. It was still on the ground when we came to the 20-foot dropoff from Roosevelt to Hazelhurst (sic) Field. I was still sitting behind, watching the ground go by and the hangars getting nearer.

When we came to the dropoff I wondered whether we would go over the ledge and settle down to the ground. Over we went and settled down, but not quite to earth. . ."[58]

The 'T-2' cleared the hangars of Curtiss Field and struggled to altitude while over much of Long Island. MacCready and Kelly were fortunate that their airplane remained airborne after traversing the ledge separating the different elevations of the two fields. A great flight attempt made in 1926 was less fortunate in this regard.

(Above) *Fokker F-VII, Curtiss Field, 1921.*

(Left) *Bert Acosta, one of the earliest U.S. aviators to fly postwar Fokker in America, cockpit of F-VII, Curtiss Field, 1921.*

(Below) *T-2 monoplane in flight, 1923.*

(Bottom) *Martin MO-1, Curtiss Field, circa 1922.*

(Above) T-2 monoplane serviced prior to flight, Roosevelt
Field, 1923. -

(Right) Fokker S-II, Roosevelt Field, circa 1923.

(Below Left) Hild-Marshonet biplane, Roosevelt Field,
1923.

John MacCready and Oakley
oplane, Roosevelt Field, 1923.

R on Curtiss Field, 1923. Note
ar.

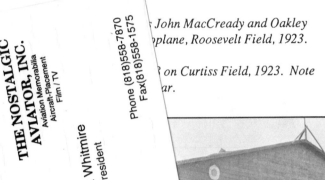

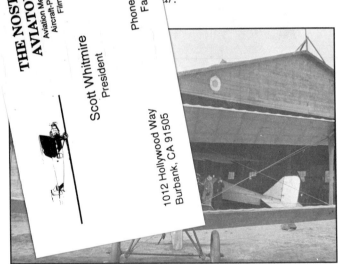

WILLIAM WAIT

WILLIAM WAIT

WILLIAM WAIT

(Top) Elias EM-2 and Boeing DII-4, Curtiss Field, circa 1924.

(Above Left) War surplus Fokker D-7 modified to monoplane and equipped with Curtiss C-6 engine.

(Above Right) DH-4 airmail carrier, Curtiss Field, 1924.

(Left) First Curtiss Lark, with Casey Jones, on Curtiss Field, 1925.

(Bottom) Laird LC-B, on Curtiss Field, circa 1925.

1926 through 1927

Sikorsky S-31, Curtiss Field, 1926.

In the spring of 1926, Sikorsky was still surviving in a dilapidated hangar on Roosevelt Field. A project already in motion (the S-35 twin-engine passenger transport), caught the attention of French ace Rene Fonck, who was in the United States making serious inquiries by which he might secure an aicraft capable of flying the Atlantic, New York to Paris nonstop, to win the $25,000 prize offered by Raymond Orteig — a weathly New York hotel owner who wished to promote aviation and brotherhood between the nations of France and the United States. The Orteig prize was first offered in 1919, and it remained unclaimed until Lindbergh. However, by 1926, the aviation community knew that an aicraft capable of flying the Atlantic was near.

Sikorsky reflected somberly on his decision to quickly modify and reluctantly forego appropriate flight tests on the S-35. He felt pressured and committed to Fonck's trans-Atlantic attempt after publicity swelled about the project's development, though he always maintained his confidence in the quality of the design had it been tested more thoroughly.

After midnight on September 21, 1926, Sikorsky himself taxied the S-35 to the east side of Roosevelt Field and supervised the airplane's fueling. The crew of four entered the S-35 around 5:00 am while Sikorsky watched from a nearby bluff:

"When the ship was about half way along the field, something happened to one of the auxiliary landing gears, which either broke or was partly released, but remained for a time attached to the plane, dragging along the ground and leaving behind a cloud of dust. A few seconds later the plane reached the end of the field, went down from the steep edge, and for a moment disappeared. Shortly afterwards a huge red flame and a dense cloud of black smoke shot up."[59]

Fonck escaped with one crew member but the others died in Roosevelt Field's most infamously spectacular blaze. The wreck of the S-35 was shocking news, but it failed to deter the quest for the first nonstop flight from New York to Paris. As Lindbergh flew from San Diego to St. Louis to New York in a hop and a dash, others were preparing to fly the ocean and more were dying while trying.

When Lindbergh landed at Curtiss Field in May, 1927, he joined two trans-Atlantic projects awaiting themselves the right moment to hop off for Paris. Of the three, Lindbergh was considered least likely to succeed; he was flying solo in a single-engine aircraft and his name was not of the stature associated with the other two camps. Lindbergh, however, was hardly an unknown within aviation circles, whether military or civilian.

In the early rain-drenched hours of May 20, 1927, the 'Spirit of St. Louis' was hitched to a wheeltruck and towed across Curtiss Field, where it was hangared, to the western edge of Roosevelt Field, where it was fueled and left poised for take-off.

Caught unaware by a late-breaking, favorable weather forecast, Lindbergh was unable to rest properly the night before the flight of his life, and it was always a source of disbelief to him that his most dangerous adversary in the course of his trans-Atlantic flight was his lack of sleep.

Perhaps 150 to 200 persons attended the Lindbergh take-off on May 20, but 50,000 people amassed on June 16, to welcome him back to Roosevelt Field. In less than a month, Charles Lindbergh had become a world phenomenon and all who knew of him also knew that his flight to Paris had begun from the muddy runway of Roosevelt Field. The unprecedented showering of adulation won by Lindbergh overshadowed everything else at Roosevelt Field during 1927, but the great flights continued, if with altered points of destination.

On June 4, Clarence Chamberlin and Charles Levine took off from Roosevelt Field in the Bellanca monoplane, 'Miss Columbia.' They landed 42 hours, 45 minutes later near Eisleben, Germany, and established a new world distance record of 3911 miles. Earlier, Levine had refused to sell the Bellanca to Lindbergh for fear of losing control of pilot selection. At one point in the flight, the 'Miss Columbia' corrected its course by estimating the distance a ship at sea had covered since leaving port, which was of value to the crew for they were in possession of a shipping schedule which allowed them to guess accurately their position. In April, 1927, Chamberlin and Bert Acosta in the 'Miss Columbia' had set a new endurance record over Roosevelt Field in anticipation of making the trans-Atlantic flight: 51 hours, 11 minutes.

On June 29, in the Fokker trimotor, the 'America,' Commander Byrd, Lieutenant George Noville, Bert Acosta, and Bernt Balchen took off from Roosevelt Field and successfully crossed the Atlantic, eventually reaching Paris though unable to land there due to fog. The 'America' subsequently alighted at sea near Ver-sur-Mer, France.

Byrd rented Roosevelt Field as his base of operations previous to his trans-Atlantic attempt. By way of courtesy, Byrd allowed both the 'Spirit of St. Louis' and the 'Miss Columbia' to use the larger field, which was more suitable than Curtiss Field for the extremely overloaded fuel-laden aircraft. Commander Byrd also constructed a ramp inclined and sloping to the west for increasing the momentum of his Fokker trimotor as it began its take-off run. The tail of the 'America' was tied by rope to the top of the incline and the link was to be severed as the 'America's' engines were throttled for take-off:

"The engines were being revved up, and I can imagine Acosta up forward in the cockpit, watching the gauge needles climb bit by bit. Suddenly the rope snaps under the pull of the big props, and we are prematurely rolling down the ramp. Acosta must make an instant decision whether to cut the switches, or gamble on gaining enough speed by the time he has reached the end of the strip. . . The end of the runway is rushing towards us, and I can picture Noville's hand groping for the dump-valve. Then, at the last split second, Acosta eases the wheel back a little, and there is a little lurch, almost a bump. The tires have left the ground."[60]

On July 1, Bernt Balchen, after 42 hours in the air, stalled the trimotor into the sea. All four crew members escaped from the 'America' unharmed, though what had once promised to be the most thorough and secure trans-Atlantic venture concluded least satisfactorily.

The last great flight to depart from Roosevelt Field in 1927 occurred on October 11, when Ruth Elder and George Haldeman in a Stinson-Detroiter, the 'American Girl,' took off at 5:04 pm. The late-season start had necessitated an alteration in the crew's flight plan due to the violence of stormy seas in the North Atlantic, so Elder and Haldeman selected a course due east. The 'American Girl' was forced to end its flight when the crew decided to alight at sea in order to secure passage on a cruising tanker. Though Elder failed to be the first woman to cross the Atlantic, she did become the possessor of the new overwater distance record of 2632 miles.

With the loss of the Roosevelt Field-based Fokker 'Old Glory' and its crew of Lloyd Bertaud, James Hill, and Philip Payne on September 7, it is no wonder that the public looked upon the Haldeman and Elder flight as an achievement—at least the two lived long enough to tell their story. But the death toll had been too ravaging and the public began to view oceanic flying as suicidal. Nobody, however, did more for aviation in the wake of 1927's successes and disasters than Lindbergh; and though Roosevelt Field never again hosted such relentless preparations as those witnessed throughout 1927, the field was finally illumined by the golden glint of world-renown.

Alexander P. deSeversky's experimental use of skis on a Curtiss 'Jenny,' Curtiss Field, 1926.

(Left) Curtiss Field office, circa 1927.

(Below Left) Sikorsky S-35, Roosevelt Field, 1926.

(Below Right) Igor Sikorsky piloting S-35, Roosevelt Field, 1926.

(Bottom) Wreck of S-35, Roosevelt Field, September, 1926.

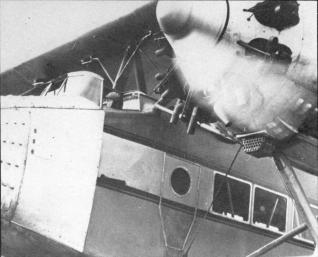

Lindbergh's Flight — 1927

AVIATION HERITAGE

(Above) 'Spirit of St. Louis' headed out over the ocean.

(Left) Charles Lindbergh standing in front of the 'Spirit of St. Louis.'

(Below) 'Spirit of St. Louis,' maintained for trans-Atlantic attempt, Curtiss Field, May, 1927.

AVIATION HERITAGE

JOSEPH BURT

(Top Left) Charles Lindbergh and 'Spirit of St. Louis,' Curtiss Field, May, 1927.

(Top Right) Charles Lindbergh and 'Spirit of St. Louis,' Curtiss Field, May, 1927.

(Middle) Engine run-up of 'Spirit of St. Louis,' Curtiss Field, May, 1927.

(Bottom) 'Spirit of St. Louis' fueled and poised for take-off, Roosevelt Field, May 20, 1927.

Guest and speaker podium, Lindbergh reception, Roosevelt Field, June 16, 1927.

Lindbergh greets motorcycle division of Nassau County Police, who supervised May 20, 1927, take-off, June 16, 1927.

MINEOLA, L. I.

NEW YORK

(Left) Ruth Elder and Stinson 'American Girl,' Roosevelt Field, October, 1927.

(Below) Wm. R. Hearst's Fokker 'Old Glory,' Roosevelt Field, September, 1927.

(Bottom) Curtiss P1-B 'Hawk,' 1926.

(Top) Admiral Byrd's Fokker trimotor 'America,' Roosevelt Field, 1927.

(Above) 'America' on Byrd's specially constructed take-off ramp, Roosevelt Field, 1927.

(Left)'America' in flight, June, 1927.

Wright-Bellanca, Curtiss Field, 1925.

Miss Columbia — 1927

(Right) Clarence Chamberlin (standing on the left) and Charles Levine, trans-Atlantic crew in 'Miss Columbia.'

(Left) Clarence Chamberlin and designer of 'Miss Columbia,' Guiseppe Bellanca, 1927.
(Below) 'Miss Columbia,' May, 1927.

(Top) Bellanca 'Miss Columbia' on Curtiss Field, May, 1927.

(Above) Test flight of 'Miss Columbia,' May, 1927.

(Left) Chamberlin, Levine, and 'Miss Columbia' en route to Germany, June, 1927.

Chapter Four

The Golden Age
1928 through 1939

View of Curtiss Field looking east, circa 1929.

1928 through 1929

Roosevelt and Curtiss Fields were the center of the aviation world in the late 1920s and early 1930s. If one stayed long enough, one was assured of seeing virtually every notable flier. Crowds flocked to see Charles Lindbergh, Admiral Byrd, Bert Acosta, Elinor Smith, Jimmie Doolittle, Roscoe Turner, Bernt Balchen, Clarence Chamberlin, Clyde Panghorn, Ruth Elder, Ruth Nichols, and Al Williams. Roosevelt Field was more than an attraction or a stage for the dashing aviators; it was the premier showcase for demonstrations of flying skill or innovative design. Curtiss, Beech, Sikorsky, Burnelli, Bellanca, Fokker, Seversky, and Grumman all displayed their latest products on the field and visiting celebrity pilots were invited to fly them. It was the capital of the air, the world's premier airport.

"Part of Roosevelt Field's charm lay in its lack of boredom. Charles Lindbergh's Atlantic flight and the successful flights of Chamberlin, Byrd and Haldeman that followed it in quick succession gave the field an aura of glamor and excitement that was absolute catnip to the

public. It wasn't long before we pilots were also swept up in the pervading atmosphere of eager anticipation, as each day brought announcements of record-breaking flights planned, cancelled, or in the making. Any place on the map that hadn't been flown to was about to be, and every hangar swarmed with the activities of preparation. We had no notion that we were watching history in the making, for all this uproar drew every promoter, con man, drifter, and fast-buck artist in the area like shavings to a magnet."[61]

After the magic of 1927, records were broken at Roosevelt Field with the fluidity of rifled calendar pages. The Curtiss Company, still in control of the western field, capitalized on the fame of its pilots and products, and it staged weekend airshows to attract crowds, sell rides, sell flying lessons, and further promote its nationwide organization. Choreographed by the firm hand of manager Casey Jones, the show was invariably a thrilling display of flying skill and danger. There were races, aerobatics, precision bombing contests, wing-walkers and parachutists. Although intended to appear to be impromptu performances, these weekend air shows were carefully contrived dances in the sky.

In 1928, a novel organization began operation at Roosevelt Field. Known as the 'Voice of the Sky' Corporation, they used Fokker and Ford tri-motors to broadcast advertisements from the clouds above. These tri-motors were modified with a trio of speakers built into the cabin area where passenger seats would normally have been. A sound-proof booth was constructed in the cabin so an announcer could read his messages into a microphone. The plane normally flew at about 2000 feet and music and announcements could be heard clearly on the streets below. Their aircraft flew primarily in the metropolitan New York area and they often advertised Cadillac and Franklin automobiles. In the absence of television advertising, promoters were always seeking new schemes to attract attention.

In an interview, June 19, 1988, with George Dade, he told of his experience:

"One company made announcements from a huge airplane that flew low over populated areas. They took out all the seats and put in three great big speakers in the center that made quite a lot of noise. But the plane had a very low gliding angle, so you had to talk fast. One day the regular announcer was sick, so the pilot, Randy Enslow, asked me to do it. I was strapped in the tail, in a wicker chair with a parachute, next to three lights— red, yellow, and green. We flew to Bridgeport, Connecticut, with the red light on which meant don't talk. When the light turned to yellow, that meant get ready with my script. At 4000 feet Randy cut the throttle so there was no noise, and we went down at a sharp angle. Then he put on the green light, which was the signal to give my pitch, and it went like this: 'At your grocer today—a free dish towel for two boxes of Silver Dust—Silver Dust—the housewife's delight.' Then I'd press a button, because by the time I got through we were right over the treetops. Randy would jam the throttle forward and we'd roar out of it, back to our altitude, and we'd do this over and over again. Imagine the flack you'd get today if you did this. Once when we were on the ground I tried to get that parachute out of the seat, but it was wedged in so tight I couldn't budge it. So I couldn't get out in the air if I had wanted to."[62]

Casey Jones, Manager of Curtiss Field, second from left, with an early Waco.

'Voice of the Sky' Fokker Trimotor with Franklin Automobile, circa 1931.

In 1928, the record flights at Roosevelt/Curtiss Field ticked on like a metronome:
* 12-14 January—Non-refueled endurance record set by Clarence Chamberlin and Roger Q. Williams in a Bellanca J, the 'A.R. Martine' - - - 51 hours, 52 minutes.
* 18 January—The world's first supercharged pursuit planes left the Curtiss factory to be flown to Wright Field for testing.
* 6 March—Charles Levine, Wilbur Stultz, and Mabel Boll in the Bellanca monoplane 'Miss Columbia' make a non-stop flight from Roosevelt

Field to Havana. This was a test flight for a planned Boll-Stultz trans-Atlantic flight which never took place. Wilbur Stultz was the pilot for Amelia Earhart's first trans-Atlantic crossing. He was killed while stunting near Roosevelt Field in 1929.

* 15 April—Colonel Arthur Goebel and Harry J. Tucker, in the Lockheed Vega 'Yankee Doodle,' established a new east-west transcontinental record flying from Roosevelt Field to Los Angeles, refueling in Phoenix; - - - 23 hours, 20 minutes.

* 28 April—The crew of the 'Bremen,' Baron von Huenefeld, Hermann Koehl, and James Fitzmaurice, arrive at Curtiss Field in a Ford tri-motor. The 'Bremen,' the first airplane to make an east to west crossing of the Atlantic, was to land at Mitchel Field after its take-off from Baldonnel, Ireland. After their rescue from the wilderness on Greenly Island, Quebec, the crew finally made Curtiss Field and New York City, where they were wined and dined for several days. While at Curtiss Field, Koehl flew the Junkers F-13, which had donated its propeller in the attempt to get the 'Bremen' off the tundra. This Junkers now had the repaired 'Bremen' prop on it, so after a harrowing Atlantic crossing, this propeller flew a leisurely 45 minutes over Long Island.

* 2-3 May—Non-refueled solo endurance record set by Lt. Royal Thomas in a Bellanca CH 'Reliance'. - - - 35 hours, 25 minutes.

* 4 May—Leonard Bonney takes off in his unorthodox Bonney 'Gull.' He reaches an altitude of 50 feet and crashes. Bonney is killed and the aircraft demolished. Bonney had used the income from his oil field in Texas to finance the design and construction of his 'Gull.' Built by the Kirkham Company in Garden City, this aircraft had the physical appearance of a sea gull whose flying ability was greatly admired by Bonney. Powered with a specially built 9-cylinder, 180 hp Kirkham engine, the plane was built at a cost of $100,000.

April 28, 1928. Arrival of the 'Bremen' crew in a Ford Trimotor at Curtiss Field.

The 'Bonney Gull' used a specially built 180 hp Kirkham 9 cylinder air-cooled engine. It was well constructed with many luxurious appointments and fittings for an untried prototype test article. Span was 40' 3", length 21' 7", weighed approximately 2,000 lbs., wing area 242 sq. ft.

The ill-fated 'Bonney Gull,' April, 1928.

Bonney designed the gull-shaped aircraft with a curved breast, tail with steerable fin, and wings in two sections connected by pulleys so they could be moved up and down or even folded back. The cockpit was enclosed in glass, had two seats abreast, and an upholstered interior. When completed, Bonney took his strange craft from Kirkham's to George Weis' hangar at Curtiss Field and soon began taxi tests. No one wanted to fly the aircraft except Bert Acosta, though, of course, he would fly anything. Bonney decided to try it himself.

"I was the announcer on the field and my job was to sell tickets for rides and to keep people at the field.

One day somebody came running up all excited and said, 'Bonney's going to fly his "Gull".' Maybe it would work and maybe it wouldn't. So on this particular day, we told people that at three o'clock the field would be closed because there would be an experimental flight. The plane had an adjustment to change the camber of the wing in flight, this was supposed to give it better performance. So Bonney took off from one corner, and you could see the whole thing because the field was wide open. He got in the air very quickly and flew up to about 150 feet. Then, all of a sudden, he must have pulled a lever because he just nosed over and went straight in. I told people to stay back, but they all ran on the field. I must say, people waited around the field just to see something like that."[63]

Charles Lindbergh with Mexican aviator Captain Emilio Carranza, in front of his Ryan Brougham, 1928. Carranza was killed shortly after.

Capt. Carranza's Ryan Brougham.

On it ticked:

* 13 July—After flying from Washington, Captain Emilio Carranza of the Mexican Army leaves Roosevelt Field on the return leg of a goodwill flight back to Mexico City. Flying a Ryan Brougham, the 'Mexico-Excelsior,' Carranza was killed when his plane hit the trees while attempting a forced landing in New Jersey during a thunderstorm.
* 20 August—Arthur Goebel and Harry Tucker in the Lockheed Vega 'Yankee Doodle' establish a new transcontinental west to east nonstop speed record of 18 hours, 58 minutes, from Los Angeles to Roosevelt Field.
* 22 August—Elinor Smith in an OX-5 Waco biplane establishes a new women's altitude record of 11,663 feet.
* 8-16 September—As part of the National Air Races at Mines Field, Los Angeles, a transcontinental Air Derby from Roosevelt Field to Los Angeles is held. Robert Cantwell, in a Lockheed Vega, was the winner with an elapsed time of 24 hours, 9 minutes.
* 14 September—Roger Q. Williams and C. Sabelli in a Bellanca monoplane, the 'Roma,' leave Roosevelt Field for Maine on a planned trans-Atlantic flight to Rome. The 'Roma' took off from Old Orchard Beach, Maine, on September 20, but returned due to engine problems and

Arthur Goebel and Harry Tucker in front of their Lockheed Vega, 'Yankee Doodle,' after record Transcontinental flight to Curtiss Field, August 20, 1928.

Elinor Smith flying her Waco under the Williamsburgh Bridge. October 22, 1928.

the flight was abandoned.

* 11 October—Roger Q. Williams and Pietro Bonelli in the Bellanca monoplane, the 'Miss Columbia,' test paraffin coated wings as a preventive measure against ice build up. The paraffin also prevents lift and the flight crashes about one mile from take-off on the Westbury Golf Course. Both survive.

* 21 October—On a bet, 17 year-old Elinor Smith takes off from Roosevelt Field in a Waco biplane and becomes the first, and only, person to fly under all four New York City East River bridges. She becomes an instant celebrity.

* 15 December—Richard James of Flushing, Queens, age 17, is awarded the 'American Society for the Promotion of Aviation Prize' for a solo transcontinental flight from Los Angeles to Curtiss Field in a Travel Air.

* 20 December—Viola Gentry in a Travel Air set the non-refueled endurance record for women, 8 hours, 6 minutes.

During 1928, the Curtiss factory adjacent to the field continued experimental development of new types for military and commercial purposes. The 'Robin' was devised, a three-place cabin monoplane, for the expanding personal plane market; the 'Falcon' mail plane was derived from the military 'Falcon'; and the 'Fledgling,' training plane made its debut flights. The 'Fledgling,' powered by a Curtiss 'Challenger' engine, was selected for use by the Curtiss Flying Service as standard equipment of its chain of flying schools. The Garden City plant also developed the XF8C-2, a two-seat fighter for the U.S. Navy, which matched the performance of most single-seaters. The craft was especially designed for aircraft carrier operations. The P3A 'Hawk' also

Bellanca K 'Roma' at Roosevelt Field, September 14, 1928, prior to aborted trans-Atlantic flight.

flew first in 1928, and Curtiss was actively engaged in continuous aeronautical research. The 'Challenger' engine was developed (a 170 hp 6-cylinder radial), and Curtiss continued its refinement of the Curtiss-Reed duraluminum propeller, the 'R' type single-piece propeller with improved aerodynamic qualities.

Plans were also announced in 1928 for the development of the Roosevelt Aviation School. The school would eventually become one of the larger civilian aviation training schools in the country. It was to have the capacity for training up to 300 students at any one time, both in flight instruction and in mechanics. This same year also saw the death of 'Merrie' Merrill, the popular manager of the Curtiss Flying Service at the field.

"'Merrie' Merrill was the second manager of Curtiss Field, and another one of my heroes. The Curtiss Company put a 'Falcon' at Lindbergh's disposal on the field and he surveyed for TAT's (later TWA's) terminals around the country. He landed at Buffalo and got fogged in, so he came back by train and left the plane there. So two weeks later 'Merrie' flew up to take the 'Falcon' back to Curtiss.

He took off from Buffalo and ran into bad weather. I was usually the last employee to leave the field so I put on the landing beacon when I left. But 'Merrie' never showed up. So the next morning we got together to form a search party and there were about 40 planes, which was the largest search party we every had. They searched four days but never found it. But a farmer later reported he heard it crash, so they went up and found the wreck.

That was the other side of aviation in the twenties. There was the romance, the excitement, the pioneering, but there was also the price of it—the blood. I used to keep this diary every night before going to sleep. I'd make a list of all the pilots who had been killed, but I stopped counting when the list reached 100."[64]

During 1929, Roosevelt Field continued to grow and expand into a major modern airport. On March 5, the field, then consisting of 391 acres, was sold by the Lanin Realty Company of Garden City, to a syndicate headed by Seth Low, financier and former Army aviator. On March 12, Low purchased Curtiss

Field and combined it with Roosevelt Field to the east, thus totalling some 491 acres. The syndicate was reorganized as 'Roosevelt Field, Inc.', and stock was issued at $18 per share.

Construction soon began in earnest as plans were announced to make this the finest airport in the country. The gully between the two fields was levelled, making the area essentially one huge airfield. Steel and concrete hangars for an additional 250 planes were built with concrete aprons 250 feet in width in front of them. Flood lights, rotating beacons, an administration building, restaurant, machine shops and service stations were also constructed. The Roosevelt Aviation School, planned to be on par with the best Army schools, was established. The Long Island Rail Road extended its tracks to bring train service right to the field. In all, some $15 million was spent on field construction. At the same time, plans were announced to create a permanent monument to Lindbergh at the field. Several thousand dollars were raised through a subscription fund, but nothing came of it.

The well-established Curtiss Flying School on the field maintained the reputation of the world's oldest flying organization. Their ground school program consisted of 24 lectures aimed toward the Department of Commerce's written pilot's exam. Tuition was $50 and it covered: theory of flight, aerodynamics, aerial navigation, cross-country flying, engines, aircraft structure and rigging, meteorology, and air commerce regulations.

There were three standardized flying courses all taught on Curtiss 'Robins' and 'Fledglings.' A private pilot's course consisting of 10 hours dual, 10 hours solo, and one cross-country flight, took six to eight weeks and cost $600. The commercial pilot's course, in order to

View of Curtiss Field looking north, circa 1929. Curtiss Factory in center.

carry passengers for hire, required an additional 30 hours of dual and solo flying and aerobatics, took some four to six months, and cost $1,300. The transport pilot's course, for all types of commercial flying, included instruction in tri-motors and amphibians, night flying, and actual experience on Curtiss-controlled airlines. It required 200 hours of flying time, took 18 months, and would cost $4,500.

Many notable records and other exciting flights continued to be made with regularity on the field during 1929:

* 30-31 January—Elinor Smith establishes women's world solo endurance record in Brunner-Winkle 'Bird.' - - - 14 hours, 30 minutes.

* 4-5 February—Frank Hawks flies non-stop from Los Angeles to Roosevelt Field, setting a new west to east record of 18 hours, 22 minutes in a Lockheed Vega.

* 27-28 March—Martin Jensen sets a world solo duration record of 35 hours, 33 minutes in a Wright J-5 Bellanca, the 'Green Flash.'

* 18 April—First flight of 'Uncle Sam,' an aircraft designed by Alexander Kaertveli, who later designed the P-47. Funded by Charles Levine as the prototype for a long-range airliner, it was powered by a troublesome Packard 2A engine. Roger Q. Williams made the first of 13 test flights. On September 20, the vertical fin became loose in flight and pilot Burr Leyson had to make a sensational spiralling left-hand turn from altitude to a ground loop landing. In the course of Levine's bankruptcy, the aircraft was sold, and was later destroyed by fire in 1931.

* 24-25 April—Elinor Smith again breaks the women's world solo endurance record with a flight of 26 hours, 30 minutes in a Wright-powered Bellanca Pacemaker. The record still stands in the U.S. The 1928 exploit under the bridges made Elinor Smith a national celebrity, and it also proved she could fly a plane with precision. In January of 1929, she had flown over 14 hours above Roosevelt Field, enough to impress and to get an offer from Guiseppe Bellanca, who was building one of the best long-distance aircraft of the day.

The Bellanca Company wanted her to break Lindbergh's 33 hour, 20 minute record for a non-refueled flight. With Bellanca flying near her in the *Daily News* plane, she flew a triangular course above Long Island with enough fuel and supplies to stay aloft for nearly two days. But a control

Noted aviator Martin Jenson prior to setting solo endurance record over Roosevelt Field in 1929.

Elinor Smith, April 24, 1929. Before endurance flight in Bellanca CH.

April 18, 1929. The 'Uncle Sam' makes its first flight. Prototype for a long-range airliner, the aircraft experienced design and flight problems and was the only one built.

cable stuck, causing the elevator to jam, and she had to come down after only 26 hours, 30 minutes—enough for the world's record for women, but somewhat of a disappointment to her. In a poll taken by the American Society for the Promotion of Aviation at the end of 1929, Smith was voted the best woman pilot in the U.S. (Jimmy Doolittle took the honors for men.)

* 15 May—Roger Q. Williams and A. Yancey in the Bellanca J 'Green Flash' start from Roosevelt Field for Maine on a planned flight to Rome. The Bellanca ground loops on take-off from Old Orchard Beach, and the flight is abandoned.

Elinor Smith, center, after being named Woman pilot of the year, 1930. Jimmy Doolittle, left, Eddie Stinson, right.

Roscoe Turner and 'Gilmore' in front of his Lockheed Air Express, Roosevelt Field, May, 1930.

* 27 May—Roscoe Turner flies from Roosevelt Field to Glendale, California, in 18 hours, 43 minutes.

* 27-29 June—Captain Frank Hawks sets a new round-trip transcontinental speed record, first flying from the field to Los Angeles in 19 hours, 10 minutes. He then turns around and comes back in 17 hours, 38 minutes. Round-trip time of 36 hours, 46 minutes. The flight was made in a Lockheed 'Air Express' monoplane.

* 27 June—Roger Williams and A. Yancey in the Bellanca monoplane 'Pathfinder' take off from Roosevelt Field for Old Orchard Beach, Maine, for a newly planned flight to Rome. 'Pathfinder' takes off from Maine on July 8 and lands in Rome on July 10.

* 28 June—Viola Gentry and Jack Ashcraft take off in a Paramount Cabinaire, the 'Answer,' in an attempt to break the endurance record of 150 hours set by an Army team in the 'Question Mark.' The next morning dense fog rolls in, and the refueling aircraft is unable to take off. Out of fuel, Ashcraft attempts a forced landing. Coming through the fog, the 'Answer' hits a large tree; Ashcraft is killed and Gentry is seriously injured.

* 1 July—Bill Stultz, the pilot on Amelia Earhart's first trans-Atlantic flight, is killed while stunting in a Waco near Roosevelt Field. It was the fourth accident within a mile of the field in one week. In all, seven persons lost their lives that week.

* 15-20 August—Nick Mamer and Arthur Walker in a Buhl CA-6 Air Sedan, the 'Spokane Sun God,' set a new endurance record. They flew from Spokane, Washington, circled over Roosevelt Field, and flew back to Spokane in 120 hours.

* 20 October—U. F. Diteman in a Warner Barling, the 'Golden Hind,' takes off from Roosevelt Field for Newfoundland for a planned flight to London. He leaves Harbour Grace on October 2 and is never seen again.

During 1929, Curtiss developed the 'Condor' B-20, a 21-place cabin biplane powered by two Curtiss 'Conqueror' engines, designed for heavy transport work. The commercial 'Condor' was adapted from B-2 'Condor' bombers. The 'Carrier Pidgeon II' was developed as a high-speed, heavy-duty mail plane, the 'Hawk' P-6 (powered by a Curtiss 'Conqueror') as a new Air Corps pursuit plane, the 'Kingbird' (an 8-place cabin monoplane powered with two Wright J-6s), for commercial use, and the 'Tanager,' a special plane powered by a 'Challenger' engine. The 'Tanager' embodied departures from conventional designs and was successfully entered in the Guggenheim Safe Aircraft Competition.

The Ireland Aircraft Company produced a five-place amphibian powered by a 300 hp Wright. The firm was soon renamed Amphibions, Inc.; and its most successful aircraft was the P-3 'Privateer,' powered by a 165 hp Wright 'Whirlwind.'

The weekly Roosevelt Field Airshow continued to expand and large advertisements appeared regularly in Long Island newspapers: *'See the Air Circus, every*

(Above) Gentry and Ashcraft's Paramount Cabinaire.

(Right) Jack Ashcraft and Viola Gentry with their Paramount Cabinaire.

(Below) June 29, 1929. Viola Gentry and Jack Ashcraft crash in their Paramount Cabinaire after running out of fuel while attempting to set new endurance record. Ashcraft is killed, Gentry seriously injured. Crash was on the site of Hicks Nusery in Westbury.

Sunday, Stunts, Aerial Acrobatics, Parachute Leaps, Bomb-Dropping, Balloon-Bursting. Plane Flights— $2.50 up. Roosevelt Field Air Circus.' No other civilian airfield in the country has ever had such thrilling weekly air shows, then or now. This was clearly indicative of the size and popularity of Roosevelt Field. The 'air-mindedness' of Americans in the 1920s and 1930s was becoming an integral part of society.

Air Transportation reported at the end of 1929:

"It is the intention of the Roosevelt Field Corporation to develop around the runways, from which Lindbergh, Byrd and Chamberlin projected trans-Atlantic flights, what promises to be the greatest seat of aviation activity on the American Continent. The development planned for Roosevelt and Curtiss Fields is too big, and involves too much capital to be built on fame alone. The program contemplates the application of all practical factors now known about aviation, with plenty of room not only for keeping abreast of progress in the industry but also for setting a pace for the rest of the world to follow.

This airport will provide every facility required in aviation, ranging from accommodations for mooring a Zeppelin overnight to the refueling of airplanes in transit. In the execution of its well laid plans the management is leaving nothing to chance. It is gathering about the field men who have recorded notable achievements in the various branches of flying.

On May 1, Curtiss Flying Service vacated and was succeeded by Roosevelt Field's own organization, built up by Nelson Kelly, an Army flier, located at Kelly Field during the war; later a mail pilot. Kelly had gathered about him a corps of experienced pilots, men with flawless records. These men

Lineup of Curtiss Commercial aircraft on Curtiss Field in 1930. All were originally developed in Garden City.

Curtiss 'Tanager,' 1929. This aircraft won the 1930 Guggenheim "Safe Aircraft" competition on neighboring Mitchel Field.

The fairly popular Privateer Amphibions (formerly Ireland) were manufactured on Roosevelt Field through the mid 1930s.

will form the nucleus of a modern system of air transport service.

The pilots will be uniformed. The planes they fly will emerge every day from machine shops manned by skillful mechanics who command such repair facilities that there will never be any reason to apologize for the condition of a plane when it is handed over to the uniformed pilot.

Up to a recent date Roosevelt and Curtiss Fields simply grew without any idea of co-ordination of activities. The various unrelated interests on the field thought themselves self-contained. Their buildings were located without any idea of co-operative effort. All that is to be changed in the program mapped out by the new management. The plan, looking far into the future, is so extensive as to demand that every square foot of the 487 acres embraced in the two fields be put to practical use.

That is the problem with which engineers of Roosevelt Field, Inc., in co-operation with a well known firm of architects are contending at this time. The position of repair shops with relation to hangars is manifestly important. Then again, it is the intention of the management that the fields shall have facilities for making any kind of repair or replacement on any type of airplane that might drop down out of the sky and ask for immediate attention.

Roosevelt Field will apply the service station idea to the airplane, with this difference—that under one roof, so to speak, there will be marshalled the facilities for giving service to any plane. This convenience is expected to give great impetus to private ownership of airplanes in the Metropolitan District. It will promote the leasing of individual hangars on the Roosevelt Fields, for the ownership of private planes will no longer be restricted to men who can afford the continuous employment of a skilled mechanic, whose actual services might not exceed a few hours each week. The individual owner who keeps his airplane at the Roosevelt Fields will be able to get immediate mechanical assistance at any time, simply paying so much per hour for the actual service performed."[65]

(Above) Curtiss 'Grasshopper,' primary glider, circa 1928.

(Right) George Dade putting parachute on Charles Lindbergh, Curtiss Field, 1928.

(Below) Brunner Winkle Bird on Roosevelt Field, circa 1928. Built in Brooklyn and powered by a Kinner engine, it was a fairly popular plane in the late '20s and early '30s.

(Bottom) Curtiss 'Condor' B-2 bomber, 1928.

(Above) Curtiss 'Condor' transport, Curtiss Field, 1929.

(Below) Curtiss 'Condor' construction, Garden City, 1928.

(Left) Cockpit of Curtiss 'Condor' transport, 1929.

(Above) Interior of Curtiss 'Condor' transport, 1929.

(Below) Curtiss 'Condor' construction, Garden City, 1928.

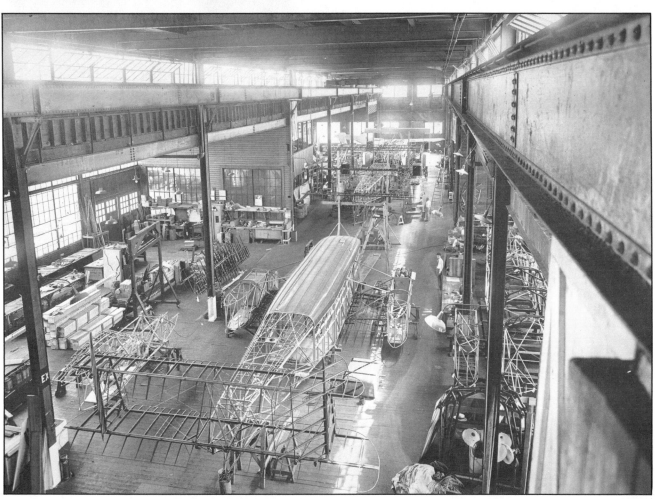

Ruth Nichols and Curtiss 'Fledgling,' 1929.

Curtiss 'Carrier Pigeon II,' Roosevelt Field, 1929.

Curtiss 'Robin,' 1929. Developed at Curtiss' Garden City plant. All production was later shifted to St. Louis.

(Top) Curtiss 'Hawk' P-6 Hoyt Special, 1929. Flight Testing on Curtiss Field.

(Above) R. Williams and A. Yancey's Bellanca "Green Flash" at Roosevelt Field, May 1929, prior to their departure for an aborted flight to Rome.

(Left) Columbia Triad. A Triphibian developed at Roosevelt Field and funded by Charles Levine. Powered by a Wright J-5, it was convertable from amphibian to either land or seaplane. Two were built, none were sold. Destroyed by a fire in 1931.

Travel Air 4-D. Used in 1930 by Aircraft Radio & Instrument Corp. at Roosevelt Field for 'Blind Flying' training.

Cunningham-Hall PT-6 on Roosevelt Field, 1929. Only two were built.

Fokker Super Universal, Elmo Pickerill, pilot. Used by RCA at Roosevelt Field for testing new radio equipment and other related research, circa 1930.

1930 through 1931

Frank Hawks' glider Texaco 'Eaglet' at Roosevelt Field after flying 2,860 miles from San Diego in 36 hours, 47 minutes in 1930.

The year 1930 saw more records being set and historic events happening on Roosevelt Field than in any other single year. This was the last year that the field served as New York's largest airport, thus it was the last time so many exciting events were concentrated there. The field was to continue as the largest civilian airport in the country for some time though. The many hangars and other field buildings were used for 150 aviation-related enterprises. Twenty different aircraft sales agencies sold virtually every type of civil aircraft on the market. There were many service concerns, repair services, aeronautical supply houses, parts businesses, and several different advertising firms. Autogiros towed banners, the 'Voice of the Sky' Corporation offered loud-speaker services. The world-renowned Roosevelt Aviation School was flourishing. The skywriters advertised products with smoke, and Fairchild Aerial Surveys took commercial photographs of the whole eastern U.S.

* January 1930—Curtiss 'Tanager,' built at Garden City plant, wins the Guggenheim Safe Aircraft Competition at neighboring Mitchel Field.

*10 March—Elinor Smith sets women's altitude record when she ascends to 27,418 feet in a Bellanca 'Pace-maker.' Later in the day she ascends to 28,416 feet. The flight almost cost her her life as she passed out at the peak of her climb, but recovered just as the aircraft began its dive.

*6 April—Frank Hawks pilots a towed glider, the 'Texaco Eaglet,' from San Diego to Roosevelt Field: 2,860 miles in 36 hours, 47 minutes.

* 9 April—Stanley Huffman flies an Aeronca C-2 non-stop from Lunkin Airport, Cincinnati, Ohio, to Roosevelt Field in 10 hours, 10 minutes. Pilot Huffman carried extra gas cans and rigged an in-flight refueling system so he could keep the gas tank full. The flight gathers some publicity and helps to promote the safety and economy features of the new Aeronca.

* 20 April—Mr. and Mrs. Charles Lindbergh fly from Glendale, California, to Roosevelt Field in a Lockheed Sirius to establish a new transcontinental record. Total flying time is 14 hours, 23 minutes, including a stop at Wichita. Average speed is 172 mph.

* 10 May—Major Alexander P. de Seversky flight tests a Sikorsky S-39 single-engine amphibian at the field.

* 17 May—World record for mass parachute jumping established at Roosevelt Field when 20 men jump from a Curtiss 'Condor.'

* 21 June—Colonel Robert Fierro of Mexico flies non-stop, Roosevelt Field to Mexico City, 2,300 miles in 16 hours, 35 minutes, in a Lockheed Sirius, the 'Anahuac.'

* 27 June—Major Charles Kingsford-Smith, with a crew of three, in the Fokker 8B-3, 'Southern Cross,' arrives at Roosevelt Field. After flying from Australia to London they flew to Port Marnok, Ireland, then to Harbour Grace, Newfoundland, and then to Roosevelt Field. An excited crowd of over 12,000 people is on hand to greet them:

"A mighty cheer roared from the vast crowd as the 'Southern Cross' came winging its way to its destination through the sunset sky, like an eagle coming down to roost at the close of day. Breaking through police lines in a wave of excited, careless humanity, the crowd surged across the field to take the fliers to its arms, while Nassau County policemen strove futilely to stem the tide.

May 17, 1930, twenty men jump from a Curtiss Condor over Roosevelt Field setting a new mass parachute jump record.

It was the greatest crowd assembled at Roosevelt Field since Nassau welcomed Lindbergh home after his historical flight that started from the same field. In size and enthusiasm it met the occasion beyond expectations.

'It was a great reception,' Captain Enequist told the <u>Daily Review</u> today. Nassau County certainly greeted the 'Southern Cross' fliers in a whole-hearted manner. The fliers themselves were surprised and pleased with the reception. Major Kingsford-Smith said he never expected such a huge crowd would meet him."[66]

* 15 July—George Pond and a crew of two in a Stinson SM-4, the 'K of New Haven,' takes off from Roosevelt Field for a non-stop flight to Buenos Aires. Near Monroe, Georgia, the plane gets lost in the fog and the crew bails out.

* 21 July—Lee Gehlbach flying a Commandaire is the first to arrive at Roosevelt Field, thus winning the last leg of the All-American Air Derby, a 7000-mile race.

* 17-30 July—Bob Black and Louis Reichers attempt to set a refueled endurance record over Roosevelt Field in a Stinson Junior. They stay up 13 days, 13 hours, failing to break the record of 556 hours set by the Hunter brothers in Chicago.

* 2 August—J. H. Mears and H. G. Brown in a Lockheed Vega, the 'City of New York,' take off from Roosevelt Field on a planned flight to Dublin. The flight is abandoned in Harbour Grace, Newfoundland, where the aircraft is damaged on take-off.

* 8 October—Laura Ingalls in a deHavilland Moth sets a new women's east to west transcontinental record, from Roosevelt Field to Grand Central Airport, California, in 30 hours, 27 minutes.

* 9 October—J. Errol Boyd and H. E. Connor in the Bellanca model 'Columbia' leave Roosevelt Field for Harbour Grace, and they fly on to the Schilly Islands, U. K.

* 18 October—Laura Ingalls in a 'Cirrus' powered deHavilland Moth sets a new women's west to east transcontinental record, Los Angeles to Roosevelt Field, in 25 hours, 35 minutes.

* 26 October—Paul Clough in an Aeronca C-2, owned by the Roosevelt Aviation School, sets a new American light plane record for aircraft weighing under 440 pounds. The tiny craft climbs to 11,800 feet.

* 28 October—Alicia Patterson in her Laird Speedwing sets a new record flying from Cleveland to Roosevelt Field in 2 hours, 41 minutes.

June 27, 1930. Major Charles Kingsford-Smith and his crew arriving at Roosevelt Field in the Fokker 8B-3 'Southern Cross.'

* 10 December—Ruth Nichols in a Lockheed Vega sets a new transcontinental speed record. She flies from Los Angeles to Roosevelt Field in 13 hours, 22 minutes.

During 1930 Curtiss concentrated its efforts on military production and on the development of huge transport planes. The company also developed the F8C4 'Helldiver,' a two-place biplane fighter and dive bomber for the U. S. Navy, and the 'Command Helldiver' with enclosed cockpits. Several experimental ships were developed: the Curtiss YP-20, a pursuit biplane with a Wright 'Cyclone' engine; the XF6C-6 racer, a monoplane with a 'Conqueror' engine; the O-16, an observation biplane with a Curtiss D-12 engine, and the YO-13C, XO-16, and O-26 observation planes. However, at the end of this year Curtiss closed the Garden City plant, which then employed 375 workers in design and experimental work. About half of these employees were shifted to the Curtiss plant in Buffalo.

Also during 1930, the Curtiss Flying Service and School moved its operations from Roosevelt Field to the new Curtiss airport in Valley Stream, Long Island. The Roosevelt Aviation School, however, was in the process of expanding its operations, so there was no lack of aviation instruction on the field.

After 1930 Roosevelt Field remained stable in size and fixed within its physical boundaries. During 1931, 55 acres in the southeastern corner were sold to the Meadowbrook Club for development into a polo field. The parcel continued to provide a convenient emergency landing field, however. During this time the field was equipped with a Sperry 1000mm floodlight in a specially built tower. The tower's roof also held a Sperry ceiling indicator, a high-intensity searchlight, and a double beacon which cast a red and white light. According to contemporaneous reports, 'this equipment makes Roosevelt Field the best lighted airport in the East.'

On August 24, 1931, Roosevelt Field became the first civil airport to establish its own newspaper. The fact that it could produce and maintain its own newspaper is clearly indicative of the extent to which operations were evolving. *The Roosevelt*

BILL WILDHAGEN

Alicia Patterson's Laird 'Speedwing,' which she used to set several inter-city speed records. Note Rhonie mural inside Hangar F in rear, circa 1936.

Ruth Nichols, a familiar face around Roosevelt Field in the late '20s and early '30s.

AVIATION HERITAGE

Roosevelt Aviation School owned Aeronca C-2, used by Paul Clough to set lightplane altitude record at Roosevelt Field, October 26, 1930.

Field News contained 'Happenings of Interest at America's Greatest Airport and Aviation Center.' It was published for the operators on the field, for pilots and students, and for visitors, and it ran weekly until 1942. Every issue noted the various pilots and companies from all over the eastern United States, who were bringing their aircraft to Roosevelt Field for servicing, alterations, or pleasure visits. People were constantly coming to the field to inspect and purchase new aircraft, or to have theirs inspected at the Department of Commerce headquarters located there. The gossip columns spoke with regularity of virtually every famous American flier who visited Long Island for one reason or another.

The weekend airshow tradition continued on the field and they regularly drew crowds in the thousands — all flocking to see the famous fliers, the airplanes on display, delayed parachute drops, and to embark upon their first airplane rides. At one time in 1931, 400 take-offs were counted within one hour. Undoubtedly, this was America's busiest airfield.

The Department of Commerce described the field in its handbook of America airports:

"Garden City—Roosevelt Field, commercial rating. One mile NE; 18 miles E of New York City. Altitude 100 feet. Irregular shape, 500 acres, sod and dirt, level, natural and tile drainage; three asphalt runways on Unit 2, all 2,000 x 100 feet; entire field also available; entire area of Unit 1 available, measuring approximately 2,500 x 2,000 feet. <u>Roosevelt Field</u> on hangar roof. Pole lines to N., E., and S., buildings to N., and E. Beacon, boundary, approach, obstruction, and landing area flood lights. Beacon, 24-inch rotating, showing alternate clear and green flashes; auxiliary code beacon flashes characteristic 'R' (. - .); facilities for servicing aircraft day and night."[67]

Roosevelt Field's other highlights of 1931 included:
* 18 March—Captain Frank Hawks in the Travel Air 'Texaco 13' establishes a new record of 55 minutes from Boston to Roosevelt Field.
* 27 March—Elinor Smith takes off from Roosevelt Field and attempts a new altitude record in a supercharged Bellanca model Skyrocket over New York City. While passing beyond an altitude of 26,000 feet the engine dies. Attempting to restart the engine, she accidently lets the oxygen tube slip from her mouth and subsequently loses consciousness. The plane glides eastward and Smith comes to at 2,000 feet. She makes a hard landing between two trees in a vacant lot.
* 9 April—Elinor Smith in a Bellanca Skyrocket reaches a new women's altitude record of 32,000 feet.
* 22 May—As a part of the 'Air Corps Coast Defense Exercises,' the Air Corps gathers an air armada of nearly every airworthy plane the Corps has, along with the ships of the National Guard. After a rendezvous in Dayton, the 672 airplanes fly to New York City and

Elinor Smith holding the barographs with CAA Representative before her first record altitude flight.

simulate a night bombing attack. On May 22, most of the ships remain either at Roosevelt or Mitchel Fields overnight. In spite of the large number of aircraft participating, and with no air traffic control, there are no accidents.
* 23 May—Floyd Bennett Field in Brooklyn opens. Now this becomes New York City's official airport. It is larger, with more paved runways, and it is closer to downtown Manhattan. Henceforth, the majority of long-distance flights start from, or terminate on, Floyd Bennett Field.
* 6 June—Bob Hall in a Gee Bee flies from Springfield, Massachusetts, to Roosevelt Field in 33 minutes, an average speed of 236 mph.
* 23 June - 1 July—Wiley Post and Harold Gatty leave Roosevelt Field in the Lockheed Vega, the 'Winnie Mae.' After eight days, 15 hours, 51 minutes—with several stops—they circle the world covering 15,128 miles. They land back at Roosevelt Field after an air time of 4 days, 12 hours.
*14 July—Captain George Endres and Captain Alexander Magyar in the Lockheed model 'Justice for Hungary' fly from Roosevelt Field to Newfoundland, then to Budapest, in 32 hours, 45 minutes.
* 18 July—James Hall, in a Lockheed Altair, the 'Crusader,' flies from Roosevelt Field to Havana in 8 hours, 47 minutes.
* 21 August—Captain Frank Hawks, in Travel Air 'Texaco 13,' establishes another record, this time flying from the field to Fort Worth, Texas, in 7 hours, 57 minutes.
* 31 August—James Hall, in the Lockheed Altair, the 'Crusader,' sets a record flying from Roosevelt Field to

View of Roosevelt Field looking east, May, 1931. Note the number of open fields around the airport.

Roosevelt Field, May, 1931. Concentration of bombers due to Air Corps 'Mass Flight' experiment.

'Winnie Mae.'

Roosevelt Field News, *June 7, 1934:*

"Wiley Post, famed round-the-world flier, arrived on Roosevelt Field Saturday afternoon in his 'Winnie Mae,' where he renewed acquaintance with his many friends. Wiley is well known on this airport, as it was the starting and finishing point for the Post and Gatty round-the-world flight. Before leaving, he had dinner with Frances Harrel Marsalis at the Roosevelt Field Restaurant. Wiley's historic Lockheed was being groomed and fitted out for another spectacular long distance flight that Fall."

New Orleans in 7 hours, 14 minutes.
* 23 September—Re-enacting the first airmail flight (which occurred in Garden City in 1911), Dean Smith flies a Pilgrim from the field over the original 6-mile route.
*27 October—Jimmie Doolittle, in a Laird Super-Solution, the 'Skyways Buzzard,' flies from Roosevelt Field to Ottawa to Washington, D.C., to Mexico City, connecting the three North American capitals. He covers 3,000 miles in 12 hours.
* 26 November—Bert Hinkler, in a 90 hp deHavilland Puss Moth, flies from Roosevelt Field to Brazil, with stops, and then on to Senegal, West Africa. He thus becomes the second man to fly the Atlantic alone.

"Of course, these record-breaking achievements were just a few of the flights which had some connection with Roosevelt Field in these momentous years. The hum of airplane motors became an everyday sound to the people of Nassau County and those who lived in the vicinity of Roosevelt were daily witnesses of innumerable take-offs and landings. While people from outside the area still came in droves to watch the activities at the field, the inhabitants of the immediate area accepted all the excitement of an airfield as being something quite natural. Because it was a suburban field there was quite possibly more activity than there would have been if the field had been more inaccessible to the general public. There were countless numbers who arrived and departed. While world records were set as has been noted, the vast majority flew for enjoyment or other purposes, but with no record-breaking purposes in mind."[68]

The field's middle years were good ones. The Roosevelt School gained an international reputation for excellence in flight and in mechanics instruction. Peak enrollment reached 1,500 and many of the students were quartered on the field, so it took on a campus-like atmosphere. In 1932, Licon Airways was established, Roosevelt's first and only

(Above) 1931 Celebration at Roosevelt Field marking the 20th anniversary of the first Air Mail flight, which also took place on Long Island. A Pilgrim was used to re-enact the historic flight, Garden City to Mineola, five miles. Pilot, Dean Smith.

(Right) Jimmy Doolittle with his Laird Super Solution, the 'Skyways Buzzard,' at Roosevelt Field, October, 1931. Doolittle later flew the same plane to victory in the 1931 Bendix Trophy Race.

scheduled airline. They flew Stinson tri-motors between Long Island and Newark, Atlantic City, Providence, New Haven, and Bridgeport. With two trips per day to each city, they were essentially a feeder line to Newark. By 1934 Philadelphia had been added to the route and the name was changed to New York Airways. This airline ceased operations in the late 1930s.

After the opening of Floyd Bennett Field the previous year, there was a complete curtailment of record-setting activities at Roosevelt, which, however, continued the most populous, busiest, and most exciting civil airport in the world. *Aero Digest* for August 1932 reported that there were twice as many airplanes at Roosevelt Field than at any other metropolitan airport. Whereas Floyd Bennett Field was mainly for commercial aviation, Roosevelt Field was mainly for the private pilot.

On August 21, James Mollison landed at the field in his deHavilland Puss Moth, the 'His Heart's Content.' He had just flown from Ireland to New Brunswick, then to Roosevelt Field. His was one of the few trans-Atlantic flights of this period. During 1932, the Department of Commerce banned all trans-Atlantic flights without specific permission and inspection by them. There had been too many fatalities during ill-prepared and ill-planned flights, so the Department decided to step up regulation.

(Left) Stinson Model A Tri-motor.
<u>Roosevelt Field News</u>, *September 24, 1934:*
"Flying from Newark last week, P. McCarthy delivered a tri-motored Stinson to Licon Airways. The ship carries ten passengers, a pilot and co-pilot. Three Tri-motored Stinsons have been purchased through a brokerage firm on Roosevelt Field for Licon to fly between Atlantic City and Providence, stopping at Roosevelt Field."

Travel Air modified by Sikorsky into a monoplane, Roosevelt Field, circa 1930.

Alexander "Bullet," circa 1930.

Curtiss 'Kingbird,' twin engine monoplane, 1930.

Burnelli GX-3. Flown by Roger Wolfe Kahn at Roosevelt Field, May, 1930. First multi-engine aircraft to feature full-span high-lift flaps as well as variable chord and camber.

Curtiss-Bleecker helicopter, Garden City-built, 1930.

1932 through 1933

James Mollison's deHavilland Puss Moth at Roosevelt Field after trans-Atlantic flight, 1932.

President of Roosevelt Field, George Orr, described the field for the June 1932 issue of *Aero Digest*:

"To insure all-weather conditions, and in addition to the fact that all the surface is high, dry and well sodded, a system of paved runways has been constructed, making possible a take-off run into the wind in a choice of ten directions. This system of runways, taxiways and aprons called for some 1,800,000 square feet of paving. The subjugation of dust was accomplished at the same time.

While Roosevelt already had more buildings and space than any other airport, an extensive program of construction was undertaken and completed, giving the airport 131,000 square feet of modern concrete and steel hangars, a new hotel, and extensive restaurant facilities. These improvements bring the buildings on the field to the unequaled amount of fifty aeronautical structures and hangar space of approximately 350,000 square feet.

On August 21, 1932, Captain James Mollison arrived to a tumultuous welcome at Roosevelt Field after his flight from Ireland in a deHavilland Puss Moth.

James Mollison getting a hero's welcome on Roosevelt Field.

There are miles of road, the main ones paved; an electric light and power system; miles of drainage and sewer piping; gas, water, and similar facilities. Some thirty-two operators carry on their business at the field, their activities ranging from the sale of gas to the manufacturing of complete airplanes.

For night flying, a most complete system of lighting has been completed, including a four-million-candle-power Sperry floodlight; auxiliary floodlights which are illuminated automatically if the arc flood fails; double-ended revolving beacon with white and green lights of three-million-candlepower and visible for more than seventy miles; a thirty-million-candlepower searchlight, ceiling finder and code beacon. The night field is outlined by border lights and all obstructions marked with red signals.

Fliers like the convenience of the field to the city, with over eighty trains a day from Manhattan and Brooklyn to Mineola, the field station, many taking only thirty-two to thirty-six minutes, or the excellent motor roads to all points. Mitchel, the large Army Field, is immediately adjacent at the south. There are twelve eighteen-hole golf courses within a radius of three miles and many open fields in the vicinity. These advantages, together with the absence of surrounding swamps and congested buildings, increase the safety of flying operations and emergency landings.

The layman who goes to the airport for an airplane ride, flying instruction or just entertainment likes the background of romance and history that pervades the atmosphere, the chance to watch the activities of those who have made and are making that history. If flying, they like the record of safety through years of operation of the Roosevelt Flying Corp. Roosevelt Aviation School is well known for its long experience, its splendid equipment and personnel, its highest Government rating and its situation. Free parking spaces for visitors' automobiles are provided right out on the flying line. By means of a public address loudspeaker system, announcements are made and events are explained to the visitors."[69]

Also during 1932 a future famed aviator began taking flying lessons in a Fleet at Roosevelt Field—Jackie Cochran:

"Husky Flewellyn is really husky, huge. He's to be my instructor. When I look over at the airplane, a little machine, and then back at Husky, I seriously question whether or not it will take the two of us up. But I say nothing.

Without a single explanation we climb into the plane, Husky opens the throttle and off we go. For some queer and unknown reason, I catch the feel of the plane right away. I had just scratched the surface, but I was less beautician and more flier already.

'How many hours do you have to fly to get a license?' I ask when we're back on the ground. 'You've got to fly 20 hours and then pass a test,' he explains. 'It'll take two or three months if you're lucky.'

'I have to do it in three weeks because I don't intend to spend my entire vacation out here,' I say. He just laughs.

'That'll be tough,' he says.

'I don't think so,' I say. And I plunk down the $495 for the course. We started putting in the hours that afternoon.

I'll never forget when Husky took me up for an acrobatic lesson with every intention of making me sick. Loops, spins, rolls, and other maneuvers in dizzying repetition. Finally, I touched him on the shoulder and pointed to the landing field. He smiled, thinking he had done his job, and we came down. When we climbed out of the plane, I invited him over to the small field restaurant, where I ordered a hot dog and a bottle of pop.

Husky Flewellyn, Chief Instructor at the Roosevelt School.

By three o'clock Monday afternoon, just 48 hours after I first climbed into a cockpit, Husky climbed out of 'our' trainer and said, 'Okay, it's all yours.'

I wanted to be the world's greatest pilot and I didn't think twice about soloing after so little time in the air. Up in the air, I was at ease, so at ease and inexperienced that I didn't worry when the motor quit. I assumed Husky had fixed it to stop so I would come down. And come down I did, with no problems. The Roosevelt people—Husky included—were amazed and quite impressed."[70]

Throughout the 1930s aircraft sales probably comprised the major business activity on the field. At any one time there were between eight and fifteen different manufacturers selling their wares. Anyone on the east coast interested in purchasing a new or used aircraft usually came to Roosevelt Field, as it had the best selection of aircraft types available. Waco was the largest distributor at the field. Its 1933 sales brochure listed Model As for $4,285, Model Fs for $4,210, and Cabin Model Cs for $5,985. Radios were $375 extra; cockpit heaters cost $15.

Several major fires destroyed parts of the field in 1933. On February 15, Hangar 6 burned and several aircraft were destroyed with total damages placed at $300,000. In June, a fire in Hangar E obliterated eleven aircraft valued at $250,000. Aircraft lost included: a Bellanca owned by Standard Oil, an Autogyro owned by

Jackie Cochran on the field, circa 1935.

Gyro Sales, a Fokker tri-motor owned by 'Voice of the Sky,' a Fleet, Stearman, Monocoupe, and a KR-34 airplane. In anticipation of raging flames the field kept as a precaution its own fire truck, stored and ready to go in an unlocked building.

Every August between 1932 and 1936, the field ran a goodwill flight to Montreal. This was one of the major social events of the season and many of the sportsmen pilots on the field took part. The event usually lasted three days, with anywhere between 40 and 75 aircraft participating. On August 19, 1933, Frank Hawks and Amy Mollison led a flight of 58 aircraft from Roosevelt Field to Montreal to attend the Canadian Air Pageant. No other airfield in the U.S. at this time ran such large social outings, which in fact further served to develop the camaraderie amongst Roosevelt's pilots and airplane owners.

The most important event of 1933 was the National Charity Air Pageant, which was held on October 7 and 8 for the relief of Depression victims. Chairing the event was Eleanor Roosevelt. Each day of the Air Pageant drew over 100,000 persons, making this one of the larger airshows in the United States. The activities in the morning included: The National Sportsman Pilot Championship for Men and Women; an International Pylon Relay Race; a World Record amphibian speed attempt; glider formation flying; deadstick stunting; and an exhibition of Marine Corps dive bombing. Afternoon events included: a mass parachute jump, speed flying in the Howard Special, 'Ike'; a World Record speed attempt by Jimmy Wedell; acrobatics by World War I German ace Ernst Udet; Autogyro maneuvers; 'Baby Ruth' races for engines up to 580 cc.; glider acrobatics; Army Air Corps bombing demonstration; delayed parachute drops; and Al Williams doing acrobatics in the 'Gulfhawk.' Evening events included fireworks aloft, jumpers with flares, and illuminated Autogyros.

Over 200,000 persons viewed the events of the Air Pageant. Edna Gardner in a Waco won the women's open race, Mrs. Cecil Kenyon won the women's amateur contest, William Zelar won the men's division; and Mr. DeFlorez won the *Scientific American* trophy for safety. Jimmy Wedell in his Wedell-Williams Racer was almost killed when a piece of the cowl broke loose and hit the propeller while the plane raced at 302 mph.

"The greatest attraction ever staged! That was the verdict today of the National Charity Air Pageant held at Roosevelt Field. A recapitulation of the two-day event showed that one world record of importance was broken. That was when Major Alexander de Seversky, former Russian War Ace, set his bronze amphibian (Sev-3) hurling through space at 177.8 miles per hour. However, the crowd of 100,000 who witnessed yesterday's final events was the largest ever assembled

National Charity Air Pageant, October, 1933. A Navy plane lays a smokescreen.

on Long Island. It got a record aggregate of thrills from the dare-devil stunts in flying and parachute jumping.

Hard luck is believed to have cheated Jimmy Wedell, Louisiana flier, out of the honor of breaking his own land speed record. On his second turn over the 3,000 meter course, he was clocked at 302 miles per hour—only 30 miles less than his record. Then a warped propeller forced him down, and he had to call off a further attempt.

Of the 30 parachute jumpers seen in action, Clem Sohn, of Lansing, Michigan, gave the throng the greatest thrill. Bailing out of a plane at an altitude of 12,000 feet, he dropped like a plummet for 11,000 feet before he yanked the rip cord. Thousands, who jumped to their feet and shrieked from the shock of it, saw the parachute finally open and land Sohn gently on the field.

While scores of planes were taken into the air, in all sorts of death-defying stunts, there was not a single crack-up and not a pilot was injured. The 'chute' jumpers were the only participants in the big show to sustain injury, when the wind blew them out of their destined courses and they landed in trees, on house-tops or in brambles far off the field.

However, the injuries amounted to no more than bruises or scratches and the exhibition hung up another record, which was for the increasing safety of aviation." [71]

After the big event was over, Jimmy Wedell remained on the field for the next couple of months. On October 16, in his Wedell-Williams racer, he set a record flying from Roosevelt Field to Cincinnati in 2 hours, 40 minutes. On November 2, he set yet another record when flying from Washington, D.C., to the field in 50 minutes.

Aerial Advertising Corporation's Keystone Bomber modified with electric sign on extended lower wing, circa 1932.

General Aristocrat, circa 1932, unidentified pilot.

1932 Cessna DC-6A owned by Federal Air Service on Roosevelt Field.

Sikorsky Standard, circa 1932.

BILL WILDHAGEN

BILL WILDHAGEN

Bob Hall's Springfield Bulldog, 1932 Thompson Trophy Racer, during a visit to Roosevelt Field.

Aviatrix May Haizlip at Roosevelt Field, circa 1933.

Two well-dressed youths ready to fly at Roosevelt Field.

Roosevelt Field was quite possibly the only airfield in the country with an on-site model aircraft shop. Here Joe Kovel adjusts his KG-1, 1933.

Waco UIC, circa 1933.

1934

The Stinson Distributor on Roosevelt Field, Hangar F, 1937. Stinson Reliants in line.

The year 1934 saw continued growth on the field. Aircraft distributors then included Bird, Lockheed, Monocoupe, Aeromarine-Klemm, Kittyhawk, Stearman, Stinson, Waco, Aeronca, Fairchild, Fleet, Standard, Aristocrat, Amphibians, Travel Air, Kellett, Curtiss-Wright, and Rearwin. Four Kellett autogyros were in operation by Gyro Sales. They daily towed banners over New York City to advertise clothes, shoes, and Irish whiskey. Despite the popular interest in autogyros they were never a business success. They were rather expensive and mechanically inefficient, so sales were minimal. Nonetheless, there were probably more autogyros on Roosevelt Field than on any other civil airport.

Roosevelt Field also upgraded its instrument and night flying capability in 1934. On April 24, the eastern leg of the Elizabeth, New Jersey, airways radio beam was re-located to pass directly over the field. Now Roosevelt was part of the airways network of directional radio beams. This made it possible to fly by radio beam from Roosevelt Field to all corners of the United States. On December 14, a two-way radio station for information and traffic control was established, WQEB. This made Roosevelt the first non-terminal civil airfield in the United States to have radio communication.

Other events of note for 1934 included: the sojourn of the Adamowitz brothers with their Bellanca model, the 'City of Warsaw,' previous to their flight from Floyd Bennett to Poland and Roger Wolfe Kahn demonstrated a new fuel known as 'safety gas' in his J-5 Sikorsky. He redesigned the aircraft's carburetion system to operate on hydro-generated non-flammable fuel.

The Third Annual Annette Gipson All-Women Air Race was held on June 24, 1934, and hosted by Roosevelt Field. The race, a 30-mile handicap around a 10-mile course, was won by Edna Gardner (Whyte), a nurse from Washington, D.C., who flew an Aristocrat. Suzanne Humphries was second in a Fairchild model and Frances Harrell Marsalis placed third in a Waco F-3. Confusion reigned for some time after the finish as eleven of the thirteen contestants made extra laps. Edith Cavis, who received the largest time allowance and was consequently the first to start, actually led the field across the finish line, but was deprived of the trophy by a post-race correction by the handicappers.

A sad event occurred in August, 1934—the death of long-time field resident Frances Harrell Marsalis.

Roosevelt Field News, April 21, 1936:

"Lou Levy, test pilot for the Kellett Autogiro Corp., arrived at Roosevelt Field Sunday from Philadelphia in a new Kellett wingless autogiro. Mr. Levy gave demonstrations to several interested people and put on an interesting exhibition of the unique flying characteristics of this new development of the giro type of craft, much to, the delight of the thousands of visitors who thronged the Roosevelt Field flying line."

Roosevelt Field News, June 7, 1934:

"The Wright powered Bellanca 'City of Warsaw,' which will attempt a flight from New York to Warsaw via Newfoundland, was christened at Roosevelt Field last Sunday by Mrs. Benjamin Adamowicz, wife of one of the pilots. A large number of Polish people drove out from New York to witness one of the most interesting ceremonies of Christening ever held at the Field. Instead of the usual bottle breaking, sixteen godfathers held sixteen streamers attached to the propeller of the plane. As the Rev. Anthony Mazurkiewixz, of Brooklyn, wished them godspeed, Mrs. Adamowicz cut the ribbons and officially christened the machine. Before and after the christening a boy's band played United States and Polish anthems.

The fliers, Ben and Joe Adamowicz, are awaiting permits from the State Department for flight. They operate the A. B. Bottling Works in Brooklyn, and have been flying at Roosevelt Field for some time. The many friends who have watched the careful preparation and exhaustive tests on and about Roosevelt Field join in wishing the fliers a safe and successful journey."

In July they made it with stops in France and Germany.

Frances Harrell Marsalis was from Houston, and after having received a small inheritance, she decided to learn to fly, which she did at the Curtiss Flying School. Thereafter, she was frequently seen about the field and was known by all the operators and by most of the pilots. With her red hair, Texan drawl, and lively disposition, she made many friends. She later became an acrobatic pilot and an airshow performer. In August 1932, she teamed with Louise Thaden and set a new women's endurance record of 196 hours in a Curtiss 'Thrush.' In December, 1933, she took the 'Outdoor Girl' to Miami and went up with Helen Richey, staying aloft for 238 hours while making the record. Afterwards she returned

(Left-Above) Annette Gipson, well-known aviatrix in the 1930s. She sponsored several all-women air races through the period.

(Left) June 24, 1934. The Third Annual Annette Gipson All-Women Air Race takes place at Roosevelt Field. Won by Edna Gardner (center with trophy) flying an Aristocrat.

to Roosevelt Field and took a job selling Wacos. She lived in a small apartment on the edge of the field and was totally absorbed in her work.

In August, 1934, she entered the first National Women's Air Meet in Dayton, Ohio. Her Waco distributor lent her her favorite flaming red Waco F-3. On August 15, during the pylon race, she was cut off by a Monocoupe and crashed to her death.

Shock and sadness blanketed Roosevelt Field. Having no family at the time, it was quickly decided to give her a royal send off. Another Waco pilot flew to Dayton to pick up her coffin and preparations were made to lay her out in the Waco hangar. The plane bearing her body was met over Manhattan by three Fleet biplanes from the Roosevelt School and from Mitchel Field came Army 'Falcons.' Frances Harrell Marsalis, dead at 29, was laid out in front of a Waco F-3 and the floor about was strewn with flowers. Everyone who knew her, both on the field and off, including many aviation greats, came to Roosevelt to view her body in state and pay their last respects. She was buried a few days later in a nearby cemetery.

The Roosevelt Aviation School was in its heyday during this time. It was the greatest civilian flying and mechanics school in the world. The School's aircraft included, among others, seven Fleet 2s, three Aeronca C-2s, and six Fairchild 71s. Major Al Williams, possessor of several speed records and an acrobatic performer, was the School's advisor and advanced flying instructor. The School offered three flying courses. The private pilot course required 17 hours of dual, 18 hours of solo flying, and 25 hours of ground school. Two cross-country flights, as well as spin practice and pylon turns were required. Total cost was $675 and loans were made of goggles, helmets, and flying suits during the training period. The commercial pilot flying course required 50 hours of dual, 125 hours of solo, flying in a cabin plane, night flying, acrobatics, and 50 hours of ground school. Total cost was $1,025. The transport pilot course included 175 hours of flying and 100 hours of ground school in the course of 52 weeks. Two long-distance flights to places like Atlanta or Miami were also required. This license allowed one to fly any type aircraft, particularly those of the commercial airlines. Students utilized heavier training ships and much of the flying was at night or on instruments. Total cost was $2,800.

Student housing and food was available in private homes for $8.50 per week, or at the Roosevelt Field Inn Hotel for $6.00 per week, plus $1.50 per day for board. Monthly tickets for New York City-bound

The 15 pilots who participated in the 1934 Annette Gipson Race at Roosevelt Field. Note Amelia Earhart behind trophy.

Women pilots prior to 1934 Annette Gipson Race.

Funeral for Frances Harrell Marsalis, August 15, 1934.

(Right) Instructor Frank Steinman dressed for flying in front of a school Fleet.

(Below) Staff and instructors of the Roosevelt Field, circa 1935.

trains were $10.56. Flight instruction at the School ran seven days a week, year-round, including night flying. They even had a placement service for graduates.

The School also ran six different mechanics courses. The apprentice course ran 24 weeks for $240 and was geared towards aircraft repair. The sheet metal course ran 24 weeks for $360 and was intended for preparation for those seeking a manufacturing career. The master course cost $480 and lasted 48 weeks. It allowed one to repair, inspect, and license aircraft. The master airplane and engine course cost $600 and ran for 60 weeks. It included the master mechanic course, plus engine repair and inspection. An airline mainte-

(Left) Al Williams (in white) with his Curtiss Gulfhawk, which was stored and maintained on Roosevelt Field in the mid 1930s. On October 5, 1935, the <u>Roosevelt Field News</u> *reported:*

"Major Al Williams introduced an entirely new and highly interesting method of group instruction last Sunday at Roosevelt Aviation School, which was equally enjoyed by the students and the many visitors at the school field. Flying his famous Gulfhawk, equipped with two-way radio, he executed a series of acrobatic maneuvers, accompanied by an interesting lecture explaining each maneuver in detail during its execution. George McCauley, of Aeronautical Radio Company, picked up the lecture over a loudspeaker to those assembled below. With a ground transmitter, he was in touch with the flier in two-way conversation at all times."

nance course covered 72 weeks. Finally, the design and construction course enabled the student to be hired as an engineer for an aircraft manufacturer. Tests for all courses could be taken on the field. The following description from the School's catalogue paints, colorfully, Roosevelt Field in the heyday of the 'Golden Age':

"Perhaps the most important factor contributing to the outstanding success of Roosevelt Aviation School is its location on Roosevelt Field, and its close connection with that great aeronautical institution. As the largest and busiest civil airport in the country, with a greater variety and number of airplanes and aeronautical busi-nesses than at any other location, the student has available a tremendously valuable asset that can be offered by no other school anywhere.

Roosevelt Field is the most famous airport in the world, not because of chance, but because of fundamental reasons and advantages which have enabled it to retain its leadership in an area of keenest competition. Millions of dollars have been expended in building many fine Long Island airports to serve the great metropolitan area, but Roosevelt Field maintains the remarkable position of housing more resident airplanes than all of them combined.

These reasons are briefly: 1) Safety; 2) Convenience; 3) Progress. Such reasons are as desirable today as when, with all the area around New York to choose from, it was originally selected. This is proved by its continued success and popularity. The exceptionally fine climatic and meterological conditions, the absence of the dangerous menace of congested buildings, surrounding water and swamps, mean everything to the flier's safety and peace of mind.

A visit to Roosevelt Field not only emphasizes its desirability as the ideal location for aeronautical training, but proves of fascinating interest to any flying enthusiast. It is a veritable City of Aviation, with a variety of aircraft and aerial activity that cannot be found elsewhere on the globe. You will find many times the number of airplanes permanently stored at Roosevelt Field than on all other airports and on a nice afternoon, especially a good Sunday, more take-offs and landings in an hour than on other fields on their busiest days.

As you approach Roosevelt Field, the entire atmosphere is one of aviation activity. A group of Army planes from Mitchel Field, the nearby Army base, is executing, with beautiful precision and grace, various maneuvers in perfect formation. The sky is dotted with private and commercial planes, open and cabin type, large and small, on every sort of business. As you enter the spa-

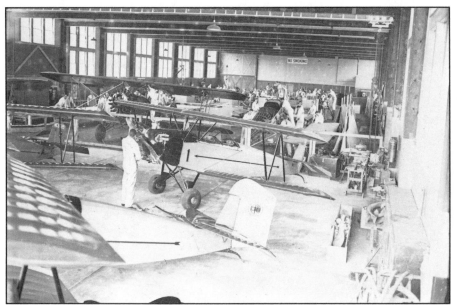

(Above) Inside the shops of the Roosevelt School, circa 1935. Students working on Fleets among other things.
(Below) Another view of the large shops at the Roosevelt School, students working on engine overhaul, welding, fabric work.

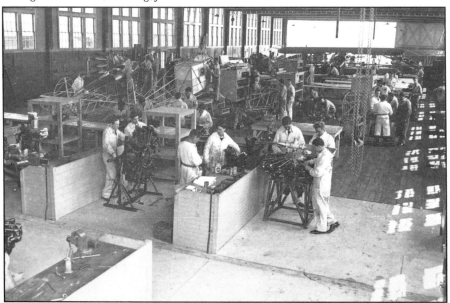

cious grounds through the main gate you are immediately conscious that this is indeed the flying and commercial center of aviation in the East. To Roosevelt Field clings that indescribable atmosphere of all that is romantic and thrilling in aviation—of daring feats of the famous who proved to the world that flying was capable of great accomplishments. It has retained that atmosphere, despite the vast program of developments that has kept it the leader of all airports.

Miles of roadways, the important ones paved, serve the more than half a hundred independent businesses conducted on Roosevelt Field. Nearly fifty buildings, including more than 300,000 square feet of hangar space, cater to every need of the flier. With many airplane manufacturers represented here, Sportsmen pilot students, who contemplate the eventual purchase of an airplane, will appreciate the ease of selection afforded by the wide variety of types on display. Advancing to the steel protective fence bordering the flying area, the visitor is amazed and delighted at the seemingly limitless flying surface, the wide concrete warming-up apron, nearly a mile and a half long, upon which are probably more airplanes in greater variety than he has ever seen before. Further out, he notes the hundreds of acres of smooth, close-cropped green turf divided by long asphalt runways, each 100 feet wide, and learns that while this is an all-turf field, take-off into 10 wind directions can be made from these paved runways. Propellers are humming and every few seconds the powerful full-throttled roar of an engine is heard, lifting a graceful plane into the air, or the singing glide of a landing ship claims attention. It is a grand, inspiring sight—to be seen nowhere else in the world. Small wonder that for more than twenty years tens of thousands have come annually to behold it!

Being interested in aviation, the

View of Roosevelt Aviation School buildings, circa 1935. Western edge of Field.

Looking north, May, 1932. Curtiss Hawks fly over the northern perimeter of Roosevelt Field.

Roosevelt Field looking south, circa 1935. Note Burnelli CB-16, Seversky SEV-3 and Waterman Arrowplane in lineup. Flight Operations building in lower right.

eager, alert young men and women, some fliers, some mechanics, claim attention. All are sun-bronzed by the healthful outdoor life and all are happy in the engrossing interest of a fascinating career. Each is highly trained and conscious of the rigid requirements of his calling. Many have completed the Roosevelt courses and are happily forging ahead with their career. Others are advance students of the School, getting the practical finishing touch to their thorough training. Even this first glimpse is enough to convince the prospective student that this is the one place to get the best aviation training.

Turning reluctantly away from the busy flying activity, one naturally wonders how and where so many airplanes are stored and serviced and how the hundreds of fliers, mechanics and airport personnel are cared for. He realizes that there is more to this enterprise than climbing into a ship and flying gaily away; that here is a really big and extremely varied business, with many millions of capital invested and several hundred persons earning their livelihood on this airport alone. Viewing the vast plant, its long 'streets' of varied buildings, hangars, offices, machine shops, laboratories, hotel and restaurant, the necessary business background of flying comes home as never before.

First a visit is paid to the Operations Office, the only building on the flying part of the field. This is 'City Hall' of this flying city, for it is from this tiny structure that administration and control radiates to all activity of the vast enterprise. Here are housed the pilots' register, the weather bureau, the post office and general administration office. First the public room in the center is entered. Here is located the information desk, presided over by an operations assistant who receives radio weather reports and posts them along with other flying information. All airport mail is distributed here and information given or arrangements made as to all activities, flying instruction and otherwise. Here also is located the telephone switchboard connecting with various parts of the airport.

Eager students overhauling a Fleet in the Roosevelt School. FRANK STRNAD

Sikorsky S-38 being maintained by Aero Trades, 1936.

To the right is the suite of three small offices of the general manager, equipped with the modern machinery of present day business. Here you learn of the surprising variety of aviation, particularly of airport management. Flying operations are only a part of the organization. A constant effort is required in sales and publicity. The utilities of a small city—streets, pavements, drainage, sewerage, fire department, police, water, gas, electric light and power must be maintained. Several hundred acres of grass, shrubs and hedges cared for; every description of building, thousands of window lights, doors, acres of roofs kept in repair; the credit and *accounting departments usual with any large realty and merchandising business provided. Engineers, draftsmen, electricians, plumbers, and carpenters are employed. The visitor learns that there is demand for all classes of workers in aviation; salesmen, stenographers, clerks, accountants, engineers, trade artisans— a use for almost every ability in the industry.*

To the left is the general accounting office and connecting with that the operation manager's office, glass enclosed on three sides, from which the flying traffic and flying operations are directed and controlled. Here you learn of the unusual flying facilities of the airport. That, already the largest civil airport in the world, more than $1,500,000 has been spent on the runways, taxiways and aprons, modern concrete and steel hangars, and a night lighting system second to none. This includes a great 4,000,000 c.p. floodlight, auxiliary floodlights, revolving double airport beacon visible for miles, code beacon, searchlight, ceiling finder, border and obstruction lights. You learn that while Roosevelt Field, Inc., administers the airport, more than fifty independent organizations give employment in every conceivable service for the airport and the flier. You learn that with such activity centered here, contacts are made throughout the whole industry.

Flight Operations building, circa 1935. Glass room on right served as 'control tower'.

Just across the paved street, in another office building, is located the modern two-way radio-telephone station, enabling the operations office to speak with airplanes flying within a radius of many miles of the airport. In this building are located one of the aeronautical service stations, a barbershop, and the general news rooms, with a number of permanent offices of national news and photographic agencies.

Flight Operations building, circa 1933. Cessna DC-6 on left, Fairchild 71 on right. Field policeman 'Scotty' Begg in center.

A further inspection takes the visitor to a handsome large building facing the flying line, the Roosevelt Field Hotel and Restaurant. This modern hostelry offers permanent and transient accommodations in single and double rooms, with or without private bath. A very fine restaurant is a valuable part of the service with lunch counter and table service in the main dining room, serving everything from soda and sandwichs to a full course dinner. A large and well appointed lobby offers a pleasant retreat for reading, cards or conversation. On the second floor, in addition to bedrooms, is a dining room, used

View of the field looking south, circa 1935.

(Above) The Roosevelt Field Inn, circa 1935. The Hotel and Restaurant stood on the northwest corner of the field and served as a gathering spot for aviators for some twenty years.

(Below) The colorful 'Art Deco' bar at the Roosevelt Field Inn, circa 1935. The aviation motif was painted by artist Eric Sloan.

as a ballroom and banquet hall, and this in turn open upon a huge tile terrace where, in pleasant weather, food and drink may be had in the open, overlooking the flying field. The hotel is perhaps the most frequented rendezvous of famous airmen in the world. Its guests include almost every flier of note, as well as an imposing list of permanent residents. Most pilots have flown from Roosevelt and return at every opportunity, sure of a welcome from many old friends.

The hangars, with their varied assortment of airplanes, prove of endless interest. There are specialists in every department of aeronautics, engine and airplane overhaul and repair stations, instrument and radio laboratories, factories, parachute packing and repair stations, propeller stations, sheet metal and welding shops, aeronautical supply houses, aerial photographers and surveyors, even public stenographers—everything for the comfort and convenience of

the flier. Not the least interesting, among all of this modern industry and activity, is the Roosevelt Field Historical Aviation Museum. In this great building is housed one of the best collections of historic aircraft and engines in the country. Beginning with an old pusher type plane of 1910 vintage, and a sister ship of the Bleriot which made world history by flying across the English Channel in 1909, the collection includes training and fighting planes, foreign and domestic, of the World War Period. There is an even larger collection of the early aviation engines. (Authors' note: This museum was the oldest pure aviation museum in the United States. The Smithsonian Institution collected aircraft earlier, but its collection was part of the Arts and Industries Museum. When the Roosevelt Field Museum was closed in 1950, several aircraft were procured by the Smithsonian, including the Domenjoz Bleriot and Baldwin's 'Red Devil.' Most of the others went to Cole Palen, who used them to establish the 'Old Rhinebeck Aerodrome' in upstate New York.)

(Top) Engine Air Service's Test Stand, circa 1935. One of many businesses on the Field. Photo courtesy Bill Wildhagen.

(Middle and Bottom)
Roosevelt Field News, August 4, 1936:

"The Aircraft Radio & Instrument Training Co., Inc. has installed its equipment in Building 13, Roosevelt Field, and is ready for business. This equipment includes an advanced Link Trainer, which simulates instrument flying in an airplane to a remarkable degree, an automatic recorder, which traces the flight path of the trainer, blind flying instruments and accessory apparatus for beams, two-way radio, etc."

There is a fellowship and comradeship about Roosevelt Field that comes of a common interest and enthusiasm on the part of all who work, study or play there. The one great interest, the dominant conversation, is flying and all that goes to make flying possible. The same indefinable influence that brings men and women fliers back to Roosevelt Field from all over the world—that makes them think of it as 'home'—soon takes possession of all who stay there. A common tie welds all into a lasting fraternity of friendliness.

As you approach the spacious modern school hangar, several training planes are usually on the line. The glistening blue fuselage and yellow wings bespeak the meticulous care given each ship in the carefully selected fleet. Perhaps a beginner is sitting in the cockpit of one, receiving last minute instructions before taking off. His helmet is fitted with earpieces through which his instructor will continue to talk to him in flight. Another solo student is just taxiing in, while others are aloft, practicing their particular problems. A class of mechanics students is clustered around an engine, undergoing live tests on a stand. There is a fine spirit of comradeship and friendliness that

(Top) *Domenjoz Bleriot in the Roosevelt Field Aviation Museum, circa 1935. This aircraft is now on display at the National Air & Space Museum. On October 29, 1935, the* Roosevelt Field News *reported:*

"A Roosevelt Field visitor of special interest last Sunday was John Domenjoz, one of the earliest exhibition fliers. Mr. Domenjoz learned to fly at the Bleriot plant in France, back in 1910. It was this same Early Bird who brought the Bleriot, now one of the most valued antiques in the Roosevelt Field Historical Aviation Museum, over to this country in 1914. Mr. Domenjoz was a test pilot for the Bleriot Company and had the plane especially equipped and rigged for upside down flying.

Visitors at the museum marvel at the equipment of this interesting plane for inverted flight, which includes heavy leather harness to hold the flier in position. They marvel no less at the daring of the pilot who attempted such maneuvers in those pioneering days, and did so with such skill that he and the plane remain intact. A few moments conversation with the intrepid Mr. Domenjoz convinces one of his fitness, and an examination of the plane discloses it to be in flyable condition today. Roosevelt Field, headquarters or host to most of America's greatest pilots, was honored by a visit from this distinguished flier and delighted to learn that he is a near neighbor, residing in Elmhurst, L. I."

(Above) *1929 Fleet 2, one of five used for flight training by the Roosevelt School, circa 1935. Photo courtesy Frank Strnad.*

immediately puts you at your ease.

Flying is taught in easy, natural stages, and each course forms a necessary foundation for each succeeding class of license. It is interesting from the very start, because the student starts flying the plane himself from the first. For this first lesson the student is assigned an individual instructor, who will give him the major part of his flying instruction throughout the course. He takes his place in the rear cockpit and the instructor explains the controls: stick, pedals, and throttle. He demonstrates how easily and naturally each movement actuates one of the three planes of control.

With these fundamentals understood, the safety belt is fastened, and helmet adjusted. Earphones for the student connecting with a mouthpiece for the instructor, known as the gosport system, permit instruction while in flight. The instructor climbs into the forward cockpit, equipped with dual controls, and taxies out into position to take off into the wind. Explaining each step, the instructor takes off while the student watches his controls and familiarizes himself with landmarks as the plane gains altitude. As his first natural tension and nervousness relaxes, he lightly grasps the controls and places his feet on the pedals. Soon he learns the sensitiveness of response to rudder, elevator and ailerons, and in a few minutes is flying along, all by himself. And what a grand sensation it is! Safe in the watchful presence of the instructor, he practices level straight flying. The instructor takes over the controls and each step in the glide and landing is eagerly watched. Imagine your own satisfaction if this were the beginning of a career of flying for you!

Each ensuing lesson has its thrill and charm, as they progress in easy stages through turns and banks, climbs and descents, until you have lost the jerky tenseness of the beginner and your maneuvers are smooth and rhythmic. Then you have the 'feel' of the air. Now follows practice on landings and take-offs, stalls and spins. Then comes the thrill of them all, you are ready for your solo flight! "[72]

George C. Dade, age 16, after he had completed his first solo flight in a Kinner Fleet airplane on July 19, 1929. Dade was the first solo student of the Roosevelt Aviation School. In the background is Hangar 16, where a little over two years earlier, Lindbergh's 'Spirit of St. Louis' had been hangared prior to his New York to Paris flight.

(Left) Gulf Executive Stinson SR-5, circa 1934.

(Below) Stinson SR-5A and Bellanca Pacemaker were among the extraordinarily diverse types of aircraft on the Field in 1934.

(Bottom Left) Lee Gehlbach with Granville Gee Bee R-6H 'Q.E.D.,' Roosevelt Field, September, 1934. This plane was built for the 1934 MacRobertson England-to-Australia Race and was unsuccessfully flown by Jackie Cochran. The plane later became the 'Conquistador del Cielo' flown by Mexican aviator Francisco Sarabia who crashed and was killed in it.

(Bottom Right) The Seversky SEV-3 on the field in 1934, with amphibian gear removed.

Forms of winter transportation, new and old, on Roosevelt Field, 1934.

A Roosevelt School Fleet equipped for winter flying. On February 17, 1934, the <u>Roosevelt Field News</u> reported:

"One of the busiest airplanes in the New York area since the snow storms is the Roosevelt Aviation School Fleet training plane which has been equipped with a set of approved skis. While long lanes of provision laden trucks remained stalled on impassable highways, this plane, chartered by the Daily News, with Chief Instructor L. H. 'Husky' Flewellyn at the controls, delivered eighty quarts of milk to the ninety snowbound sick children at the Nassau County Sanatorium near Farmingdale. The blanket of snow covering Long Island provided an excellent landing area directly in back of the hospital, making it possible to deliver the milk right to the door of the institution."

Crack-Ups

(Right) Piper Cub in an unusual landing attitude, circa 1940.

(Above) Unknown type aircraft crash, circa 1935.

(Left) Taperwing Waco after runway collision, circa 1936.

(Right) Bird Model CK, circa 1935. Unhappy pilot on left.

(Middle) Apparently the same Bird after previous, or another mishap.

(Bottom) A Fleet evidently after encountering a pole, circa 1935.

(Above) A Curtiss 'Fledgling'
destroyed by fire, circa 1932.

(Right) The remains of a Taylor Cub
after a mid-air collision, circa 1934.

(Bottom) Fairchild 22 gathering a
crowd, circa 1932.

Travel Air E-4000 stands on its nose, circa 1935.

A Roosevelt School Fleet 2 after a forced landing, 1934.

(Above) An unknown aircraft type goes up in flames. The Field CAA Inspector "Dome" Harwood usually did the investigation of all Field crashes. It was an unpleasant job:

"Lots of times I'd have to go to the crash. Awful? Oh, geez. One night we were over at my boss' house in Westbury, my wife and I, when I get a call, bad crack-up at Roosevelt Field. We go over there, this experimental airplane, there were three guys in it, coming in for landing, they just spun in, geez, all three guys burned up. We go back to my boss' house, his wife is upset because we're late for dinner, and we walk into the dining room and what does she have on the table but a great big roast beef. I took one look at that, and that's all I could stand. I'd just been looking at these bodies all burned to a crisp." (Dade & Vescey, _Getting Off the Ground_, Dutton, 1979)

(Left) A Curtiss 'Robin' in the slush, 1932.

(Left) A Stinson SR pilot gets a hand out after an unusual landing. About such accidents, the Roosevelt Field News stated in July, 1935:

"The pell mell rush out on the flying field last Wednesday when a student turned a plane over on its back was about the most perfect demonstration of foolhardy disregard of even elementary common sense safety, to say nothing of Field Regulations, that we have ever seen. An accident that caused no injury might have been turned into tragedy by a thoughtless rush of curiosity seekers streaking out on the flying area in utter defiance of landing planes. Men supposed to know better acted like a lot of children.

There is no way to police such a situation, unless the management is forced to the disagreeable and certainly unwelcome extreme of arresting violators. To control the thoughtless and impetuous who will not think for themselves we must depend upon the operators and cooler heads. All gates and barrier chains closing openings in the flying area fence should be closed at all times, except when a plane is actually passing through. Operators can and should see to that. And when anything does happen on the Field, all who are interested in preventing injury are requested to cooperate by stopping those others who would go rushing madly across the runways."

(Left) Even Autogiro crashes were not that uncommon. Here a Kellet K-4 comes up short. Circa 1934.

(Below) The Dade Co. picks up another wreck.

1935 through 1939

Aviatrix and artist Aline Rhonie painting her mural 'The History of Aviation on Long Island' on the wall inside Hangar 'F', 1935.

During 1935, Aline 'Pat' Rhonie, a noted Long Island artist and flier, decided that someone ought to document the varied and important aviation history that transpired at Roosevelt Field and vicinity. Thus, she took it upon herself to create a huge mural, in fresco, portraying the history of aviation on Long Island, focusing on Roosevelt Field, and including all noted events, significant flights, and the important aircraft and personalities. She began her mural on a 1,500 square foot wall of Hangar 'F' at Roosevelt Field, and when completed, 36 months later, it depicted over 600 aviators and 268 types of aircraft, covering the period 1909 through 1927. The tedious fresco style of painting involved drawing each line nine times and used five coats of plaster. Ms. Rhonie worked on the 120-foot long mural 10 to 14 hours a day, six days a week, in a drafty and unheated hangar. Fortunately, the mural still survives today and it is on permanent loan to the Cradle of Aviation Museum, Garden City, New York, where it will serve as a lasting tribute to formative years at Roosevelt Field. Ms. Rhonie personally brought over an Italian art expert in 1960 to remove and save the mural just before Hangar 'F' was demolished.

In 1935, the Department of Commerce subsidized the development of inexpensive 'safety planes' to promote civilian flying. It was intended to develop an automobile of the air, which anyone could fly with ease, and would be as cheap as a car. It was a wonderful idea, but the reality of it proved somewhat more difficult. Nonetheless, two of these novel planes were based at Roosevelt Field for a period of time during 1935. These were the Waterman 'Arrowplane' and the Stearman-Hammond Y-1. Both aircraft embodied design features which made them easier and safer to fly; both had tricycle landing gear and were resistant to spins. They proved to be relatively easy to fly, but they were slow. Both were pusher designs, which have inherent aerodynamic problems. In the pusher, the propeller is always operating in air previously disturbed by the fuselage and wing, and is thus less efficient. However, both aircraft utilized the design to permit better visibility, similar to that of an automobile. Only one of each was built under this program, but they did attract a fair degree of attention while at the field.

Roosevelt Field News, October 15, 1935:
"The most interesting plane on Roosevelt Field last week was Waldo Waterman's unique Arrowplane, which he flew here from Washington. This is the most successful of the planes developed for the Bureau of Air Commerce in its efforts to encourage a low priced, supersafe plane for the general public. It is a radical departure from conventional design, being a two-place, side-by-side tail-less cabin plane, of the pusher type. While still purely experimental, it possesses many extremely interesting characteristics and all were interested in Mr. Waterman's demonstrations over the weekend."

Another Department of Commerce "Safety Plane" on the Field in 1935, the Stearman-Hammond Y-1.

Roosevelt Field News, December 17, 1935:
"Everyone is interested in examining the light French designed airplane, the 'Pou-du-Ciel,' or the 'Flying Flea,' just brought over from England. The tiny machine, of which some 100 have been built and are flying in France and England, was assembled and rigged by the students of Roosevelt Aviation School and taken for its first American flight last week by Clyde Pangborn at Roosevelt Field."

Business was booming on the field. The Roosevelt Aviation School and the Safair Flying School offered courses for all pilot grades. One of the bigger commercial concerns on the field was Air Associates, which manufactured a line of flying clothes and special aircraft accessories. The firm also acted as a distributor for foreign manufacturers of aircraft, engines, and accessories.

In December, another unusual aircraft arrived at Roosevelt Field, a tiny French "Pou-du-Ciel" or "Flying Flea". This aircraft was then enjoying widespread popularity in Europe as an inexpensive, easy to fly, home-built aircraft. Unfortunately, the design proved to be extremely dangerous and unstable, and in some cases fatal. It never became popular in the United States, but the first one, which was demonstrated at the field by Clyde Panghorn, did gain a degree of notoriety.

There was one other unusual, but dramatic, event at Roosevelt Field in 1935. While flying, Jean Ellis, a New York socialite learning to fly at the Roosevelt Aviation School, had the throttle of her Fleet get stuck at full open. For 45 minutes, the 22 year-old banker's daughter flew over the field, unable to land. On the ground a sign was hastily painted on another aircraft: "If throttle stuck, cut switch when I wave hand." Her instructor went aloft to lead her to a safe landing and to show her when to cut the engine to land in the proper place. It was her seventh solo hour. She followed the instructions imprecisely, cut the switch too late, and overshot the field. She ducked in the cockpit as the plane hit a fence and flipped over. She then unbuckled her belt, dropped from the cockpit unhurt, powdered her nose, and blithely walked away.

On February 26, 1936, the Hempstead Town Board petitioned to change the zoning for the eastern portion of Roosevelt Field (Unit No. 1) for the construction of an automobile racetrack. This change involved 242 acres and included the runways from which all the 1927 trans-Atlantic flights were made, as well as the R-34's mooring and the 1923 Fokker T-2 take-off.

There had been relatively little flying on the old field as it was exclusively used for a practice take-off and landing area by students. There was only one hangar on

Curtiss 'Fledgeling' used to help get down Jean Ellis safely in 1935. As neither aircraft was radio equipped, a flying sign was needed.

the old field and it was used by the Bureau of Air Commerce and the Roosevelt Aviation School. As early as 1927, and through the early 1930s, there was talk of establishing some sort of monument to Lindbergh on the site of his take-off. To this day, nothing marks the location.

The *Roosevelt Field News*, February 12, 1936 reported on the sale of the land in positive fashion:

"After a meeting of the Contest Board of American Automobile Association, Captain E. V. Rickenbacker, Chairman of the Board, announced the approval of plans for the construction of an automobile racing course, and sanction for international racing classics, on that part of Roosevelt Field known as Unit No. 1. A company, Motor Development Corporation, has already been formed with adequate capital of over three-quarters of a million dollars to finance the construction of the racing plant.

Every protection will be given the flying facilities of Roosevelt Field. George W. Orr, President and General Manager of Roosevelt Field, states that one of the important parts of the contract between the two corpo-

rations is that no obstructions will be placed upon the field other than in a fence at an angle of more than ten to one. Any obstructions in a ratio of twenty to one will be properly lighted. The race course, which will be a four mile road course, will not take any of the area from Unit No. 2, upon which all buildings and facilities are located, other than the Roosevelt Aviation School hangar and the night lighting equipment. Unit No. 2 will be adequately lighted for night flying and the school will be moved to Unit No. 2. A separate practice field will be maintained at a distance from Roosevelt Field for its flying students.*

All who have heard of this project are convinced that it will mean a great deal to the development of Roosevelt Field, as well as to Nassau County, generally. The new plant has been pronounced by Captain Rickenbacker the finest and most spectacular racing plant in the world and, at the same time, the safest. In the two or three events that will be run each year, persons will be brought from all over the world to see the international competition planned for the track. The racing classics scheduled will be to road racing what Indianapolis is to track racing. All of the operators on Roosevelt Field will share in the increased interest and advertising that the airport will get and from increased business it will bring to the Field."[73]

By July, Unit No. 2 was completely outfitted with new night lighting equipment. This included boundary and obstruction lights, rotating beacon, lighted wind tee, and Sperry floodlights. In this way, Roosevelt Field remained one of the better equipped night flying airports in the United States.

On January 13, 1937, the old wooden Aero Trades

Roosevelt Field News, November 4, 1937:

"Major Alexander deSeversky, President of Seversky Aircraft Corp., Farmingdale, arrived at Roosevelt Field Sunday in his single seater Seversky low wing monoplane (AP-1). This airplane is powered with the double row Pratt & Whitney geared 1,000 hp Wasp engine and Major Seversky will leave shortly in this airplane for a trip to Mexico City and South American countries."

hangar, which dated to 1917, burned to the ground in 30 minutes. On July 16, Edward Maloney piloted an all-metal twin-engine Barkley Glow monoplane on a record 2 hour, 10 minute flight from Detroit to Roosevelt Field. The 550-mile distance was covered at an average speed of 250 mph. Another speed record was set on May 19, 1938, when Alexander de Seversky flew a Seversky AP-1 monoplane from Roosevelt Field to Washington, D.C., in a record 58 minutes. It was an otherwise quiet 18 months until July 1938, when Roosevelt Field experienced its event of greatest infamy.

On July 10, a young Irish-American named Douglas Corrigan piloted his 9 year-old decrepit Curtiss Robin on a non-stop flight from Long Beach, California, to Roosevelt Field in 27 hours, 50 minutes. Corrigan

Douglas Corrigan at Roosevelt Field, July, 1938.

(Middle) Roosevelt Field News, July, 1938:
"Douglas Corrigan arrived at Roosevelt Field Saturday from Long Beach, California. Douglas made the trip here in his Curtiss Robin in 28 hours, non-stop. The plane contained only a small number of instruments and no radio. During his stay here the airplane will be stored with Reich Air Service, Roosevelt Field."

(Below) Roosevelt Field News, August 9, 1938:
"Douglas Corrigan, who astounded the World by his solo flight to Dublin, Ireland, was at Roosevelt Field Sunday and called on Steve Reich who was Doug's host on his arrival from California. Doug was introduced over the public address system to a large crowd of spectators by W. D. "Jim" Guthrie, President of Roosevelt Field Inc. His Curtiss Robin monoplane was brought to Roosevelt Field Monday from New York by George Dade and the wings, which were damaged, are now being repaired by advanced students of Roosevelt Aviation School."

Roosevelt Field News, March, 1939:
"Douglas Corrigan, well known trans-Atlantic flyer and now a movie star and author, has purchased a Wright J-5 Ryan monoplane from Thorwald Johnson, Inspector for the Civil Aeronautics Authority at Roosevelt Field. Doug arrived here Sunday in his new ship and left the same day for Washington, D.C. He will start shortly on a tour of 14 states, ending at the San Francisco World's Fair, where his famous Curtiss Robin monoplane is on exhibition."

The Brewster XSBA-1 was assembled and test flown on Roosevelt Field in 1936. It was the only one built. However, it was the first of many Brewster aircraft to be tested on Roosevelt Field.

originally purchased the Robin for $900 and had it re-engined with a used Wright J-6 engine purchased at Roosevelt Field. The old plane lacked a radio and modern instrumentation, and its speed from California averaged 97 mph. The locals on the field were incredulous that Corrigan had flown it all the way from California non-stop, actually assuming he had flown in from nearby Long Beach, Long Island. When word leaked about what he had done, there was a brief flurry of publicity for the small fellow in the leather jacket who had flown non-stop across the country in a nine year-old crate with a minimum of instruments.

Brewster F2A fighter being shipped by Dade Bros. from Roosevelt Field in 1939.

Corrigan stayed at Roosevelt Field for a week, during which time he repaired his oversize gas tank, secured new maps, and generally puzzled field personnel. In the early morning hours of July 17, Corrigan took off from Roosevelt Field for nearby Floyd Bennett, from where he stated his intent to fly non-stop back to California. Corrigan wanted to leave from Floyd Bennett due to the longer runways there, as his heavily loaded plane would need as much room as possible just to get off. At Floyd Bennett, Corrigan filed a flight plan back to California, and officials there had some doubt he would make it in the old plane. Corrigan took off from Brooklyn and 28 hours, 13 minutes later he arrived in Dublin, Ireland. "Wrong Way" Corrigan always claimed he got mixed up in the clouds and simply flew in the wrong direction. Nonetheless, in the straits of the Depression,

America was sorely in need of a good laugh and "Wrong Way's" flight made him an instant hero and engendered world-wide sentiments of goodwill. When Corrigan returned to Roosevelt Field later that summer, he was mobbed by well-wishers and autograph seekers, and given a big dinner at the Roosevelt Field Inn.

Rounding out 1938, in an early season snow, was Mark Heany's unique landing. On November 28, Heany landed his Fairchild model cabin monoplane on Roosevelt's snow-covered runway. This landing was unusual in that the aircraft was equipped with floats, and

Alexander deSeversky owned two American-built Savoia Marchetti S-56 amphibians, which he had maintained at the Roosevelt Aviation School. Here one sits in the school building, circa 1937.

Warren Merboth in his Bowlus Glider on the Field after completing a flight of 200 miles from Elmira, New York, July 2, 1939. He flew the distance in 6 hours, 20 minutes, to win first prize in the "goal flight" of the National Glider meet in Elmira.

it used the floats as skis. This was the first landing of its kind at the field. In December, Hilda Ya-Tsing Yen earned her pilot's license at the Roosevelt School. She was one of China's first women pilots. She then toured the U.S. speaking on behalf of Chinese war relief.

With Europe on the brink of war, the American military machine began its build-up and made its presence felt on Roosevelt Field. Contracts were signed between the Roosevelt Aviation School and the Army to train mechanics for the Air Corps. In August, 1939, the first crew started, 200 men at a time. Eventually, over 1,200 students were trained for the Air Corps — taught, housed, and fed on a three-shift schedule. The Brewster Aeronautical Corporation of Long Island City also took over one hangar for the final assembly and flight testing of its F2A Buffalo fighters.

During 1939, New York City opened its new municipal airport at North Beach, Queens, soon to be known as LaGuardia Airport. The new airport was closer to the city than Floyd Bennett, so all commercial activity shifted there. No airlines used Roosevelt Field for any purpose other than small repairs and equipment installations. Roosevelt, however, still remained one of the larger civil airports in the world. Just a partial inventory of the aircraft repaired for the public during 1939 at the Roosevelt School shows the amazing diversity of aircraft then on the field. In 1939, repairs were made on: Curtiss 'Fledgling,' American-Savoia, Fleet, Ryan, Curtiss 'Robin,' Waco, Aeronca, Aristocrat, Thrush, Grumman F3F, Curtiss-Wright 'Junior,' Stinson, Brunner-Winkle 'Bird,' Pitcairn autogyro, Fairchild 21, Fairchild 24, Beech 'Staggerwing,' Great Lakes, Travel Air, Monocoupe, Fairchild 71, and Curtiss 'Hawk.'

Two events of minor note occurred on Roosevelt Field during 1939. On January 16, the Bulgarian Assen Jordanoff experimented with a system for freezing airplane fuel to reduce fire hazard in the event of a crash. Using a 'Fledgling' biplane, he kept the gas at 100 degrees below zero centigrade by using dry ice. The fuel was gradually warmed through a special device while going through the fuel line. The device, however, achieved no practical usage.

On July 2, Warren Merboth, a German-American glider pilot, flew a Bowlus glider 200 miles from Elmira, New York, to Roosevelt Field to win the goal prize of the National Glider Meet in Elmira. The flight took 6 hours, 20 minutes.

The most important event on the field for the year took place on July 27. On that day Bill Lear gave the first public demonstration of his new automatic direction finder (ADF).

"Bill Lear's new automatic direction finder was demonstrated to the press and five news reel companies last Wednesday. A yacht, equipped with two-way Lear transmitter-receiver combination, with the press representatives aboard, was cruising somewhere out on Long Island Sound. James B. Taylor, who has the new Automatic Direction Finder installed in his Fleetwings Amphibian, took off from here and tuned in on the yacht. Immediately the direction finder automatically spotted the location of the yacht and Mr. Taylor flew over the ship in a total lapsed time from here of 10 minutes after take-off. This conclusive demonstration will be shown in all the news reels throughout the country." [74]

The Lear automatic direction finder, as developed at Roosevelt Field, later became part of the standard instrumentation on all commercial airliners and on many private planes.

Even as World War II approached, Roosevelt Field was still the busiest purely civil aviation field in the United States. Roosevelt's general manager issued the following 24 regulations:

1.   All air traffic shall circle the Field to the left and outside of the safety limits of the Field, which are: Motor Parkway to the South and West; Long Island Rail Road to the North; and an imaginary line from East side of polo field to hangar on Unit No. 1 to the East.

2.   No turns shall be made within the above boundaries, either to right or left unless to avoid accidents, whether in taking-off or approaching for landing. It is the responsibility of the pilot to look carefully to all directions before making any turns.

3.   All take-offs and landings, when practical, must be directly into the wind, as indicated by the main control wind tee and at a safe distance from buildings and areas reserved for the public.

4.   Pilots must taxi via safe route to point of take-off, observing planes in the air and planes or other objects on the ground, and must remain off runways or landing area, facing line of approach until clear.

5.   Planes must not remain on runways or landing areas after landing is completed, but pilots must maneuver planes to observe approach and landing area before starting to taxi to flying line or point of take-off and must keep well clear of all landing planes and planes or other objects on the ground.

6.   No aircraft shall be flown under 1,000 feet altitude within the boundaries described above, except in taking-off and landing or to avoid accidents.

7.   No take-off is permitted when the ceiling is reported to be less than 500 feet, unless planes and pilots are equipped for blind flying.

8.   Avoid taking-off over residences near the airport or flying over congested areas whenever possible. Do not fly over Mitchel Field and avoid contact with airplane traffic at Mitchel Field.

9.   No landings on or take-offs shall be made from any of the concrete warming aprons, and no landings shall be made on the asphalt taxi strips that join and are parallel to the concrete apron, except in cases of emergency.

10. After taking off, all planes shall proceed in straight flight until beyond the boundaries of the Field, except in cases of emergency. All turns should be left turns, with the line of traffic.

11. A plane approaching the Field, as from a cross-country flight, shall join the traffic and circle to the left with it before landing.

12. Engines shall not be run or warmed up at any other place than the concrete aprons on the flying field. A licensed pilot or mechanic must be at the controls and chocks placed under the wheels or parking brakes set before starting engine. Chocks must be removed from the concrete aprons when not in use.

13. Airplanes shall not be taxied across roadways or from hangars to concrete strips. The roadways and auto parkway spaces shall not be used for parking planes.

14. Airplanes shall be parked with tail towards the field, except when wind conditions make it impractical, with wheels on the outside edge of the concrete, except on wide concrete aprons where painted line is shown.

15. Airplanes shall not be serviced with gasoline while the motor is running, nor refueled in hangars, roadways, or auto parking spaces.

16. Visiting pilots are requested to register at the Field Operations Office immediately after landing, and check out immediately before leaving. Weather reports are available at Operations Office.

17. While the Management maintains lighting for night landings and endeavors to keep the flying area in safe condition and flags dangerous spots as they occur, it assumes no responsibility for damage to persons or airplanes on account of the failure of lighting facilities or the condition of the Field. It is the responsibility of the pilot to observe the condition of the Field and avoid landing in water, soft spots on the Field or any other obstacle that may cause damage.

18. All airmen operating on or over this Field shall use precaution to avoid accidents.

19. No person is permitted on the landing area, taxi strips, or warming up aprons without special permission from an official of Roosevelt Field, except operators, passengers, pilots, mechanics and others having business there.

20. The towing of banners, powerless gliders, etc., will not be permitted to or from the Field without special permission from the Management.

21. Avoid congestion by using back roadways and observe 'No Parking' signs and use caution in driving. No automobiles are permitted on the landing area, taxi strips or warming up aprons, except in case of emergency, without express permission from an official of Roosevelt Field.

22. Concrete aprons outside of the chain barriers on the Field side of new concrete hangars shall not be used by automobiles, either for driveways or parking.

23. Smoking in hangars is prohibited. All persons on the property shall exercise the utmost care to guard against fire and prevent injury to persons or property.

24. Gasoline shall not be brought on the premises or stored in hangars or other buildings, except by express permission from an official of Roosevelt Field.

February 1, 1939

W. D. Guthrie
General Manager

W. D. "Jim" Guthrie, President of Roosevelt Field on right, with a Beech Staggerwing, circa 1935.

Roosevelt Field News, November, 1938:
"The Spencer-Larsen cabin amphibian, built in Farmingdale, arrived at Roosevelt Field Thursday, piloted by P. H. Spencer, President of the company. Test flights from the land will be conducted over the next few days. Water and speed tests have been conducted from Port Washington in the past ten days. The trim little job has many unique features, principally the landing gear and pontoon combination, as well as the motor location in the hull and shaft propeller. No production plans have been announced."

(Left) In the mid 1930s, the advanced Burnelli CB-16 lifting body transport stayed on the Field for awhile. It was often flown by Clyde Pangborn (right).

(Below) 1939 Bellanca 28-92 Long Distance Racer at Roosevelt Field. Powered by a Ranger and two Menascos, it placed second in the 1939 Bendix Race. Art Bussy, pilot.

(Above) Cardinal Pacelli arriving at Roosevelt Field in a Boeing 247 in 1936. In 1937 he became Pope Pius XII.
(Top Left) DC-2 of Canadian Colonial Airways visiting the Field for some radio gear installation, 1939.
(Left) Brewster F2A fighter being worked on at the Field, 1938.

Roosevelt Field News, October 5, 1937:
"The first airplane built by the Gwinn Aircar Company of Buffalo, New York, was flown to Roosevelt Field Saturday by Mrs. Nancy Love, sales representative for the Company. This new type airplane which, compared with the conventional model, is revolutionary in design, attracted the attention of a large crowd of spectators. The airplane is powered with a 90 hp geared Pobjoy Niagara engine, it is a two-place side-by-side biplane, has a cruising speed of 101 mph and it is claimed that the gas consumption is 21 miles per gallon. The airplane has no rudder, and in flight, turns are made by turning the steering wheel to right or left. The manufacturer claims that the Aircar will fly, fully loaded, with complete control and maneuverability at 41 mph." In 1938 Frank Hawks was killed flying this aircraft.

(Above) _Roosevelt Field News_, September 1936:

"W. K. Vanderbilt's new Sikorsky S-43 amphibian was flown to Roosevelt Field from Bridgeport, Conn., Friday by his pilot Earl White. The plane was delivered without upholstery and will be completed at Roosevelt Field to Mr. Vanderbilt's special specifications. This ship is designed to carry eighteen passengers and a crew of three, but will have special arrangement for private use."

(Left) _Roosevelt Field News_, October 5, 1940:

"Miss Gloria Swanson, the well known motion picture actress, came out to the airport last week to christen the 'Win with Wilkie' Bellanca Monoplane. This airplane, which is equipped with 'Voice of the Sky,' a loud speaker device, will tour the New England states urging voters to cast their ballots for the Republican Presidential nominee."

(Bottom) One of several Grumman Gooses on the Field in late 1930s.

(Above) _Roosevelt Field News_, October, 1937:
"W. K. Vanderbilt's twin engine Douglas amphibian, flown by pilot A. Caperton, arrived at Roosevelt Field last week to transact some business. This ship is one of the few which can be taken along on a yacht and used as an aerial tender. Mr. Vanderbilt has had a special cradle prepared on the after deck of his private yacht, 'Alcor,' and the large amphibian can be taken right aboard. It is understood that the yacht and plane will leave shortly for Miami and from there will start a long cruise through the South Seas."

(Center) _Roosevelt Field News_, December, 1936:
"The value of having an aviation unit as a necessary part of a complete equipped police force was very clearly demonstrated last week when the Nassau County Police Department's Stinson Reliant, piloted by Lieut. Jack Witney, was assigned to search for a truck which had been missing for 36 hours. The plane circled over Nassau, Suffolk and Queens counties for about three hours before sighting the vehicle in the dense woods north of Bethpage. There is no telling how long it would have taken to locate the truck had the search been conducted by automobile."

An unusual Vultee used by Pratt & Whitney for experimental work at Roosevelt Field, 1939.

(Top) *Lockheed Electra 10A, circa 1937. Several Electras were kept on Roosevelt Field including Harold Vanderbilt's.*

(Above) *In 1939, Clare Bunch, President of the Monocoupe Co. flew this modified plane from California to Roosevelt Field, non-stop.*

(Left) *Kellet KD-1 on the Field, 1936. Roosevelt Field always had a surprising number of autogiros on hand.*

(Below) *Texaco Executive Lockheed 18 Lodestar, 1939.*

<u>Roosevelt Field News</u>, January 14, 1936:
"Laura Ingalls, who has gained much fame for herself and her
fellows of the fair sex, by many accomplishments in the air,
arrived at Roosevelt Field with her speedy Lockheed Orion and
will make her flying headquarters at this airport for an indefinite
period. Miss Ingalls has made Roosevelt Field her headquarters
for much of her brilliant flying carreer and is cordially welcomed
back 'home' by her many friends and admirers."

(Above) Flying in style in a Monocoupe 9A, circa 1938.

(Right) Amelia Earhart during a 1936 visit to Roosevelt Field in
her Lockheed Electra.

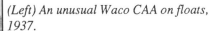

(Left) An unusual Waco CAA on floats, 1937.

(Center) Roosevelt Field News, August 4, 1936:
"The Daily News has purchased a Jacobs powered cabin Waco from Waco Sales of New York. This plane, especially constructed for aerial photography, is equipped with complete blind flying instruments, radio and night flying equipment."

(Below) A Waco YOC being used for aerial photograhpy, circa 1936. John Drennan and crew shown.

June, 1936. 279 Army Cadets stay at neighboring Mitchel Field for Air Corps basic training. They train on Keystone LB-6 bombers, which become a frequent sight over Roosevelt Field during that period.

The only Air Ambulance on the east coast flew out of Roosevelt Field in 1939 and 1940. Frank Steinman operated a modified Cessna T-50, ferrying patients to hospitals dealing in special types of cases.

(Right) Speedy Ryan ST on the field, 1937.

(Below) Roosevelt Field News, March 14, 1936: "Russel Thaw, of Garden City, arrived Thursday flying a Northrop Gamma 2-H monoplane in which he streaked across the United States at a speed of 240 miles an hour. Not trying to establish a record, he covered 1580 miles from Amarillo, Texas, to Roosevelt Field, non-stop, in 6 1/2 hours, while his flying time from Los Angeles was 11 hours, 5 minutes. This Northrop is equipped with 715 hp Wright engine, Sperry robot pilot, two-way Western Electric radio, full blind flying instruments, and flaps which reduce landing speed to 55 mph. A top of 224 mph and a cruising speed of 205 is claimed. Mr. Thaw had the advantage of a 35 mile tail wind, but was forced to fly blind for two hours through a dust storm."

(Bottom) Seversky AP-7 and EP-1 being prepared for shipment to South America at the Dade Plant, 1939. The Dade plant was located on the northwest corner of Roosevelt Field.

(Above) Laird Speedwing, circa 1935.

(Left) Bellanca Skyrocket, circa 1935.

(Below) Modified Stinson SR-5 used by the Daily News for aerial photography, circa 1935.

(Across Top) Beech Staggerwing B17R, owned by Aerial Explorations of Long Island City for Aerial mapping, circa 1935.

(Across Bottom) Aeronca C-3 sits in front of hangar row, circa 1935.

Roosevelt Field News, August 27th, 1935: "Gerd Achgelis, famous German stunt pilot who has come to this country to give exhibitions at the National Air Races, Cleveland, Ohio, was a visitor at Roosevelt Field last Sunday. The enormous crowd of Sunday visitors at that popular airport were thrilled by the spectacular exhibition he gave them. Flying his Focke-Wulf Stieglitz biplane, he used his whole bag of aerial tricks, including inverted stunting and a beautifully executed assortment of aerobatics. He left for Cleveland Monday where he will put on his excellent exhibition as a feature each day of the show."

(Left) 1934 Stinson SR-5 Reliant. The first aircraft owned by the Nassau County Police, it was kept on the Field.

(Below) Taylor E-2 Cub with a Szekely engine and a Waco 10 sit on the Field after a rainstorm, circa 1935.

Dr. Albert Forsythe and his Lambert Monocoupe, "Booker T. Washington," during a 1934 visit to the Field. Between 1933 and 1935, Forsythe made a series of long distance flights through North and Central America to popularize aviation to the black community and to inspire black youth to see aviation as a new avenue for advancement.

Roosevelt Field's resident parachutist was Joe Crane, left. He jumped regularly at the weekend airshows for years. Here he adjusts the harness on a budding jumper, circa 1935.

Frank Hawks and friend in the "Sky-Chief" on a 1935 visit.

Closeup of Jack Wright's Monocoupe on the Field. They did not win the 1934 MacRobertson Race.

(Top) Jimmy Wedell in his Wedell-Williams Racer attempted to set a new World speed record at the 1933 Air Pageant.

(Above) Frank Hawks and his Northrop Texaco "Sky-Chief" was a frequent visitor to Roosevelt Field between 1933 and 1935.

(Left) In the late 1930s, well known exhibition pilot Al Williams kept his Grumman "Gulfhawk" (modified F3F) on Roosevelt Field. It was maintained by the Roosevelt Aviation School and he used the Field as his base of operations.

Arrow Sport V-8. A distributor for these new aircraft opened on the Field in 1935. It was the first aircraft sold with an auto engine. Built as a Department of Commerce "Safety Plane," 100 were sold for $1,500 each.

Alexander deSeversky with his record-setting SEV-3 amphibian on the field. He visited Roosevelt Field frequently between 1926 and 1939.

(Top Left) September, 1935. Felix Waitkus and his Lockheed Vega visits Roosevelt Field prior to his attempted flight to Lithuania. He crashed in Ireland.

(Top Right) Al Williams and modified Grumman F3F "Gulfhawk," Roosevelt Field, circa 1937.

(Left) Unknown well-dressed aviatrix in front of Stinson SR-5, circa 1935.

(Below) Unknown aviatrix at Roosevelt Field, circa 1935.

Two unknown women fliers ready to try out the Gregor GR-1.

(Top Left) Roosevelt Field News, August 17, 1934: "Michael Gregor, the first man to build and fly a successful airplane in Russia and who has made a great contribution to American aeronautical engineering, notably on the all-metal Army pursuit ship PW-4 and the Seversky Amphibian, has a new 90 hp two-place airplane which he has developed over the past three years and expects to market for $1500. Mr. Gregor plans to begin manufacture of the plane, for which a good many orders have already been received, as soon as necessary arrangements can be made, and in the meantime is demonstrating it from Hangar B."

The fairly popular Privateer Amphibions (formerly Ireland), were manufactured on Roosevelt Field through the mid 1930s.

Boeing 247-D, circa 1935.

Chapter Five

World War II to Present

The Spartan Executive dealer on Roosevelt Field, 1940.

In spite of the opening of several new airports in the greater New York area, Roosevelt Field maintained its leadership as the premier airfield for the private flier. At the end of 1940, there were still 272 planes based on the field, making it the largest non-military or commercial airport in the world.

Without question, mobilization for World War II financially bolstered Roosevelt Field. The field, however, was too far from Manhattan to become a success commercially, and the closer fields were larger. In the 1930s, there was tremendous residential development in the field's vicinity. In the late 1930s, the first of what would eventually become a torrent of noise complaints and protests about the field appeared in local papers. Newly settled suburbanites were adverse to the noise and the occasional aircraft dropping into their backyards. Community dissatisfaction, along with the fact that private flying never expanded to the extent predicted and the field subsequently provided little tax revenue, made Roosevelt Field's future bleak.

With the approach of World War II, however, activity on the field increased. Now the field began to change its focus from private flying to military and mechanical training. The Roosevelt Aviation School not only trained mechanics for the Air Corps, but its civilian students were also quickly employed by the growing defense industry. Most of the School's graduates stayed on Long Island to work in the burgeoning defense plants there. These included Grumman, Republic, Brewster, and Sperry. The U.S. Navy leased five hangars on Roosevelt Field in 1940 in order to modify U.S. aircraft destined for England. In 1940-41, Brewster F2A Buffalos and Grumman F4F Wildcats were a common sight at the field. As most of the aircraft were heading for England, 125 British military personnel were stationed at Roosevelt to oversee the shipments. In 1941, Dade Brothers of Mineola contracted to modify the aircraft for the British. Grumman F4Fs, Brewster F3A 'Corsairs,' and Chance-Vought F4Us were repainted in British markings, had their radios replaced with British ones, and the Corsairs had their wings shortened to fit in the lower clearance of British aircraft carriers. During the war, Dade Brothes modified some 500 aircraft of all types.

The increased military business of 1940 allowed Roosevelt Field, Inc. to pay its first dividend — 20¢ a

The Abrams Explorer, built as a wide visibility aerial survey photo plane, stayed on the Field for part of 1940.

Republic RC-3 Seabee being shipped by Dade Bros., 1946.

share. Apparently the first and only airport to have shared a dividend, payments continued on a regular basis throughout the war. The neighboring automobile racetrack was less fortunate. Roosevelt Raceway declared bankruptcy in 1940, and the land was leased for the construction of a harness racing track.

By 1941, the majority of activity on the field was military in nature. Wildcats were being shipped to the British, and Buffalos were being test flown for the U.S. Navy. Dade Brothers started a major business crating and shipping aircraft from Roosevelt Field, both for the United States and for foreign governments. Corsairs, Buccanneers, and Wildcats appeared on the field in droves to await crating and shipment overseas. At several times during 1941, civilian pilots on

(Above) Vultee P-66s being packed for shipment overseas by Dade Bros., Hangar F, 1941. Note Rhonie Mural on far wall.

(Right) Republic P-43 Lancer getting ready to go, 1941.

(Bottom) A Dade Bros. caravan of Brewster Buffalos, circa 1941.

A diverse collection of aircraft being prepared for shipment to the Dutch and British in 1941. These include Beech AT-11, Curtiss P-40 and Vultee P-66.

(CAP). The CAP was given two hangars on Roosevelt Field and the use of several former privately-owned aircraft. In these planes, the CAP began anti-submarine patrols off Long Island. The *Roosevelt Field News* for December 16, 1941, reported:

"We are a long way from being back to normal. Conditions being as they are, it is extremely doubtful if we will ever again see things moving as smoothly as they were prior to that 'Fateful Sunday.' The re-adjustment is going to be slow but it is going to be steady and already enough progress has been made to make it possible to take some of the flying out of the Inn and put it back in the air." [75]

Roosevelt had their planes confiscated by the government for national defense purposes. Virtually all multi-engine aircraft, especially Lodestars and Electras, were seized for this reason. The aircraft eventually became military transports for personnel and cargo.

When the Japanese attacked Pearl Harbor on December 7, 1941, the shocking reverberations were felt at Roosevelt Field immediately. On December 9, the Civil Aeronautics Administration issued orders suspending the certificates of all civilian pilots in the United States, except for those involved with the airlines. It was feared that aircraft might be used to bomb U.S. defense establishments. As a result of this issuance, all private flying on Roosevelt Field ceased, and this condition remained for the duration of the war.

On December 14, Beckwith Havens, an early aviator and a Fairchild distributor on the field, was named head of the New York State Civil Air Patrol

The end of private flying on Roosevelt Field also terminated the need for private repair work. The Roosevelt School shifted its entire operation to the training of Air Corps mechanics. Throughout the war, the School ran 24-week instruction programs in general maintenance work.

The Civil Air Patrol still flew private planes from the field and at times six planes were in the air at once on anti-submarine patrols. The CAP's aircraft were mostly model Stinsons or Fairchilds. Since no private flying was permitted, the military ordered the removal of propellers from Roosevelt's inactive private fleet. The U.S. Navy also confiscated privately owned aircraft from the field, particularly all Grumman 'Goose' amphibians.

On February 3, 1942, the last issue of the *Roosevelt Field News* was published:

Gulf executive Lockheed 18, circa 1940.

Civil Air Patrol member on Roosevelt Field, 1943.

"The management of Roosevelt Field regrets to announce that this issue of the _Roosevelt Field News_ will be the last one published for the duration of the war. This action is necessitated by the lack of really worthwhile items of interest caused by the regrettable, but necessary, curtailment of private flying and the fact that it is not desirable in these times to publicize the movements of those privately owned airplanes whose operation is still permitted.

The first issue of this little four page sheet was put out August 24, 1931, and regularly every week since then it has gone out to interested readers all over this country and in many foreign lands. It has carried news of local and national interest concerning world famous personalities in aeronautical circles, all of whom have at one time or another described Roosevelt Field as their home airport. Perhaps its greatest appeal, however, was found in the human interest stories of happenings in the lives of the tenants, operators, pilots and employees on the Field.

Now its voice will be stilled, for how long—no one can tell."[76]

The _Roosevelt Field News_ was never again published.

Through 1943-44, the only action on the field was military. The few private planes allowed to fly could only make flights in service of the military, such as ferrying defense executives about. All civilian planes on the field were propellerless and others were ordered to leave. Many of the aircraft were sold or flown to smaller fields further out on Long Island. Most never returned. The Roosevelt School was forced to sell its five Fleet airplanes as they no longer served any purpose.

During this time, the Dade Brothers became directly involved with aircraft production at their factory on the northwest corner of Roosevelt Field. They were awarded a contract to build the wooden wings for Waco CG-4 troop gliders. Using a work force comprised of a large percentage of women, Dade Brothers turned out 720 sets of glider wings during the war. Many of these gliders were used in the invasion of France in June, 1944. In addition to building gliders, the

Between 1940 and 1945, the Navy leased several hangars on Roosevelt Field for the preparation and shipping of aircraft for overseas. Many of these were Grumman F4F-3 (G-36) "Martlets," pictured here, for the British.

Roosevelt School Aircraft were available for use by Naval aviators, circa 1942.

Morse Code instruction to Naval radiomen, Roosevelt Field, 1942.

Dade Brothers were given the reponsibility to crate and ship entire CG-4s overseas. Long caravans of gliders could now be added to the list of military planes being crated and shipped from Roosevelt Field.

At the end of the war, in 1945, military activities on the field came to a halt. There were no more crates and shipments; no more mechanics being trained for the U.S. Army Air Force. Roosevelt Field suffered from the dispersal of its former fleet of private ships, and from the dismal postwar civil aviation market. At the end of 1945, Roosevelt Field, Inc. sold the raceway property to the Raceway Corporation, effectively reducing its land to the 250 acres of the airport. The liquidation sale of Roosevelt Field was imminent.

Activity at the Roosevelt Field was modest after the war. Robinson Airlines briefly operated a ferry service to upstate New York in the late 1940s, but the venture was a failure financially. There was some private flying on the field, and storage and overhaul activities continued. Under the G. I. Bill, the Roosevelt School continued to train mechanics, but the interest in aviation generally was considerably less than what it had been in the 1930s. Often, there was talk of plans to make Roosevelt Field into a major overhaul and repair center,

as well as a base for feeder transport and cargo lines, but nothing came of it:

"I kept waiting for Roosevelt Field to get back to normal, but of course it never did. All that flat space that made Long Island the 'Cradle of Aviation' was now being used for housing developments. We heard that Bill Zeckendorf was going to plow over the old airfield and put up a shopping center at Roosevelt Field. I pleaded with them to save Hangar 60—the old Moisant hangar—to keep it for a museum, but nothing doing. They just tore it down and put in a parking lot." [77]

In January, 1949, the Roosevelt Aviation School permanently closed its doors. What was once the greatest aviation school in the country was forced to close in its 20th year of operation due to the termination of the G. I. Bill. Without the support of government-paid training, the School could no longer attract enough students to remain solvent. In March, 1949, the Roosevelt Field Inn went bankrupt. Again, without flying activity the Inn was unable to remain open as a viable attraction.

On October 8, 1949, Roosevelt Field hosted the celebration for the 50th anniversary of Nassau County. A plaque was dedicated in commemoration of the 'world's premier airport':

"Within the half century that has marked the life and growth of Nassau County, one of its leading industries—aviation—has also reached an eminent position in the fields of civilian economy and the maintenance of international peace.

This worthy accomplishment reflects credit on all who have labored long and hard to advance the cause of aviation in every way. But there is a special expression of gratitude due to those who, in the early days of flight on Long Island, contributed their skills to the development of the aeronautical sciences and to the acceptance of the airplane as a vital means of communication between peoples and between nations.

To these, Long Island's pioneers in aviation, the people of Nassau County pay tribute during this Golden Jubilee celebration for having given so much of their time and their efforts toward making Long Island the Cradle of American Aviation in a very real sense.

Dedicated October 8, 1949;

Some of the Naval personnel stationed in the militarized Roosevelt Field, 1943.

One of many Vultee P-66 fighters flown to Roosevelt Field for shipment overseas, 1941.

Dade Bros. workforce poses in front of one of the huge wooden CG-4 Glider wings, 1944.

(Above) A complete Waco CG-4 glider leaves from Roosevelt Field. They were used in Europe for the D-Day invasion.

(Right) Waco CG-4 glider wings under construction at the Dade Bros. plant adjacent to Roosevelt Field, 1944.

Roosevelt Field—Scene of countless historic flights."

The plaque, like the field, has since disappeared.

In August, 1950, Roosevelt Field was sold to Webb and Knapp. In its early days, the field's suburban location ensured its success; but by mid-century frequent protests from the surrounding and fast-growing residential communities were voiced, particularly in regard to low flying planes and the concomitant danger of crashes. Though Roosevelt Field failed to maintain its solvency, it had never shown an operating loss for all years between 1936 and 1951.

In May, 1950, the wake for Roosevelt Field was held at the Inn. Over 200 persons, including local plane owners, operators, Quiet Birdmen, friends and neighbors, gathered one last time to bid a sad and sentimental farewell. Few eyes in the house remained dry.

"An aviation landmark is passing away, due to the pressure of New York's expansion. Roosevelt Field, scene of the take-off of Col. Charles A. Lindbergh on his famous trip to Paris 23 years ago, and many other noted flights, will become an industrial site in central Nassau County in a few months. Nostalgia notwithstanding, the end of this historic field as an active airport was inevitable. Nassau's extreme postwar growth was anticipated and the county's officials had prepared for it."[78]

A forlorn looking Roosevelt Field, 1946. Four visitors gaze quietly at an Ercoupe and Budd Conestoga.

In October, 1949, Nassau County held its Golden Anniversary celebration at Roosevelt Field.

A rather sad looking DC-3 sits outside the defunct Roosevelt School, August, 1950.

BILL WILDHAGEN

On May 31, 1951, the Roosevelt Field runways were officially closed. Perennial policeman on the field, Sargeant "Scotty" Begg, painted a 20 foot long white 'X' on the main runway signifying closure. The fifty or so remaining airplanes were flown to Long Island's smaller fields. The ceremonious last and lonely take-off was performed by Roosevelt Field's first operations manager, Mr. J. Nelson Kelly. Around the field was posted:

"To all aircraft owners, operators and pilots of Roosevelt Field— I have been instructed to inform you that all flight operations will cease at Roosevelt Field on June 1, 1951. After this date there will be no facilities such as boundary and obstructions, storage or tie-down, hangar service or other services in connection with flight operations, and the Field will be closed for such operations. Any take-off and landings after this date will be entirely at your own risk. W. D. Guthrie, President."

A postscript landing and take-off from Roosevelt Field occurred later in 1951. On October 10, as part of an industrial show, a Fairchild C-120 packplane, the "Flying Bloodmobile", was flown in to dramatize the need for blood during the Korean War.

On October 6, 1951, Hangar 16, in which Charles Lindbergh stored the 'Spirit of St. Louis' in May, 1927, was demolished. Calls to save the building as an historic monument were unheeded.

The Roosevelt Field Shopping Mall opened in 1956. At the time it was one of the largest shopping centers in the United States. In September, 1960, Aline Rhonie's historical mural was removed from the wall of Hangar F by Professor Leonett Tintori, and was successfully preserved for the enjoyment of future generations. Among other things Hangar F became "Captain Video's Spaceworld," an unsuccessful amusement center; and later

Hangar 16, the hangar in which Charles Lindbergh's plane was stored, being demolished, October 6, 1951.

A view of the austere Roosevelt Field Shopping Mall, looking northeastward, 1960. Note the three remaining hangars along the north edge of the field.

it served as storage space for municipal buses. From 1964-1967 Hangar A was used as a disco known as "Murry the K's World." The night club was infamous for the raids made on it, given its reputation for serving liquor to minors. Three of Roosevelt Field's concrete hangars were standing as late as 1971:

"In a few years they will be gone, replaced by still another motel or office building on the inaptly named Old Country Road. But for now, the three decrepit structures are still there, testifying simultaneously to the glorious dreams of some men and the less glorious dreams of others."[79]

Two years later the three hangars were demolished for another commercial construction project.

In May, 1947, Bill Odom and the A-26 "Reynolds Bombshell" visited Roosevelt Field. He later set a solo around-the-world speed record.   BILL WILDHAGEN

The last landings on the site of Roosevelt Field (long after the Field was closed) were made during 1968 when the shopping center held a "Salute to Aviation." Here, landing in the parking lot, is a 1929 Arrow Sport, then owned by John Talmadge.

Roosevelt Field looking south as it looks today. It is hard to imagine that there was ever such a wonderful airfield here. Now the site is just one of a plethora of Long Island shopping malls.

Footnotes

CHAPTER ONE

1. Smith, Henry Ladd. Airways: The History of Commercial Aviation in the United States. New York, 1942.

2. 'An Epitome of the Work of the Aeronautic Society from July, 1908, to December, 1909', Bulletin No. 1, reprinted November, 1958.

3. Roseberry, C. R. Glenn Curtiss. Garden City, New York, 1974.

4. Loening, Grover Cleveland. Monoplanes and Biplanes. New York, 1911.

5. Hempstead Sentinel, 15 July, 1909.

6. Roseberry.

7. Ibid.

8. Willard, Charles. 'The Exhibition Years'. Journal American Aviation Historical Society, Fall 1974.

9. Hempstead Sentinel, 23 September 1909.

10. Walden, Henry. 'A Day in the Life of a Pioneer'. The Sportsmen Pilot, 15 March 1938.

11. Ibid.

12. New York Times, 2 June 1910.

13. New York Times, 21 August 1910.

14. New York Journal, 16 September 1910.

15. Aeronautics, November 1910.

16. New York World, 29 September 1910.

17. New York Times, 1 October 1910.

18. Aircraft, May 1911.

19. Aero, 13 April 1912

20. Brochure: 'The Moisant Aviation School', 1911.

21. Flying, October 1912.

22. Jerwan, S. S. 'The Story of the Old Moisant School'. The Sportsmen Pilot, 15 December 1938.

23. Ibid.

24. Ibid.

25. Ibid.

26. Aircraft, June 1913.

27. Aircraft, July 1913.

28. Aircraft, May 1913.

29. Ibid.

30. Oakes, Claudia M. United States Women in Aviation through World War I. Washington, D.C., 1985.

31. Aero and Hydro, 10 January 1914.

CHAPTER TWO

32. Paine, Ralph D. The First Yale Unit: A Story of Naval Aviation 1916-1919. Cambridge, 1925.

33. Elliot, Stuart E. Wooden Crates and Gallant Pilots. Philadelphia, 1974.

34. Ibid.

35. Letter in the collection of the Cradle of Aviation Museum, Division of Museum Services, County of Nassau, New York.

36. Ibid.

CHAPTER THREE

37. Air Scout, 15 July 1919.

38. Ibid.

39. Ibid.

40. Letter in the collection of the Cradle of Aviation Museum, Division of Museum Services, County of Nassau, New York.

41. Foxworth, Thomas G. The Speed Seekers. New York, 1971.

42. Leary, William M. Aerial Pioneers. Washington, D.C., 1985.

43. Bowers, Peter M. Curtiss Aircraft : 1907-1947. Annapolis, 1987.

44. Brochure: 'The Curtiss Aeroplane and Motor Company,' 1920.

45. Aircraft Year Book, 1921.

46. Ibid.

47. U.S. Air Service, September 1921.

48. Aircraft Year Book, 1926.

49. Aircraft Year Book, 1928.

50. Matt, Paul R., and Foxworth, Thomas G. 'Curtiss PW-8.' Historical Aviation Album, 1971.

51. Brochure: 'The Curtiss Aeroplane and Motor Company,' 1926.

52. Aircraft Year Book, 1924.

53. Brochure: 'The Skywriting Corporation of America,' 1923.

54. Related by Elinor Smith Sullivan, 1988.

55. Sikorsky, Igor I. The Story of the Winged-S. New York, 1958.

56. Ibid.

57. Aircraft Year Book, 1922.

58. Casey, Louis S. The First Nonstop Coast-to-Coast Flight and the Historic T-2 Airplane. Washington, D.C., 1964.

59. Sikorsky.

60. Balchen, Bernt. Come North with Me. New York, 1958.

CHAPTER FOUR

61. Smith, Elinor. Aviatrix. New York, 1981.

62. Interview: Mr. George Dade and authors, 19 June 1988.

63. Ibid.

64. Dade, George, and Veosey, George. Getting Off the Ground. New York, 1979.

65. Butler, Frank. 'Historic Roosevelt Field.' Air Transportation, 18 May 1929.

66. Nassau Daily Review, 27 June 1930.

67. U.S. Department of Commerce. Descriptions of Airports and Landing Fields in the United States, 1931.

68. Stubbe, Barbara. 'The Story of Roosevelt Field.' Nassau County Historical Society Journal, Volume 24, No. 3, Summer 1963.

69. Orr , George. 'Roosevelt Field.' Aero Digest, June 1932.

70. Cochran, Jackie, and Brinley, Maryann, Jackie Cochran. New York, 1987.

71. Nassau Daily Review, 10 October 1933.

72. Catalog: 'Roosevelt Aviation School,' 1934.

73. Roosevelt Field News, 12 February 1936.

74. Ibid, 1 August 1939.

CHAPTER FIVE

75. Ibid, 16 December 1941.

76. Ibid, 3 February 1942.

77. Dade and Veosey.

78. New York Times, 16 August 1950.

79. Newsday, 21 June 1971.